Risk Management for Nonprofit Organizations

Risk Management for Nonprofit Organizations

Rick Nason
Omer Livvarcin

BEP BUSINESS EXPERT PRESS

First published in 2020 by
Business Expert Press, LLC
222 East 46th Street, New York, NY 10017
www.businessexpertpress.com

ISBN-13: 978-1-95152-722-8 (paperback)
ISBN-13: 978-1-95152-723-5 (e-book)

Business Expert Press Finance and Financial Management Collection

Collection ISSN: 2331-0057 (print)
Collection ISSN: 2331-0049 (electronic)

Cover image licensed by Ingram Image, StockPhotoSecrets.com
Cover and interior design by S4Carlisle Publishing Services Private Ltd., Chennai, India

First edition: 2020

10 9 8 7 6 5 4 3 2 1

Printed in the United States of America.

Dedication

We would like to dedicate the book to all the volunteers and professional managers who serve in nonprofits in order to improve their communities and the lives of their constituents.

Abstract

This book positions risk management as a key element in successfully managing a nonprofit organization. Risk management in nonprofits has several unique characteristics that distinguish it from risk management in for-profit organizations. This book presents and explains specifically tailored strategies and tactics for risk management in nonprofits.

This book is a straightforward, yet comprehensive, guide that can be used to easily communicate effective risk management ideas among the various stakeholders who comprise a nonprofit organization. This is a book that can be used to educate and inform nonprofit professionals as well as the nonprofessional volunteers who are so critical to the operations of many nonprofits. It is a tool that will enhance both understanding and communication of risk management principles.

Written in clear, jargon-free language, it is a resource that can be read by board members, professional nonprofit managers, volunteers, and other stakeholders of the nonprofit organization. As a tool for building a common appreciation and understanding of risk management, this book has the potential to become a valuable asset for the nonprofit organization.

Keywords

risk management; nonprofit organizations; governance; enterprise risk management; risk decision making; risk assessment; risk mitigation; risk frameworks; regulation; strategic analysis; risk measurement

Contents

Introduction ....*xi*

Chapter 1   What Is Risk? What Is Risk Management? 1
Chapter 2   Basic Principles of Risk 17
Chapter 3   Risk Management Frameworks 31
Chapter 4   Risks of Nonprofit Organizations....................................45
Chapter 5   Risk Analytics 59
Chapter 6   Financial Risks 75
Chapter 7   Operational Risks...89
Chapter 8   Legal, Compliance, and Reputational Risks...................101
Chapter 9   Risk Treatment...113
Chapter 10   Partnerships and Stakeholder Engagement 133
Chapter 11   Risk Governance 149
Chapter 12   The Future of Risk Management......................................163

About the Authors...*173*
Index *175*

Introduction

Why Nonprofits Need Risk Management

This is a book outlining ideas and processes for implementing risk management in nonprofit organizations. It is quite reasonable to ask why such a book is required. We believe that there are many reasons for such a book, and after reading the book we hope that you will agree.

The first reason is that all organizations, whether for-profit or non-profit, can benefit from risk management. We believe that risk management has many benefits to bestow on all types of organizations. Risk management, as outlined in our approach, helps organizations achieve their strategic goals. In addition, it helps to prevent threats to the organization as well as capture opportunity. We state here clearly and emphatically that risk management is simply good management, and all nonprofit organizations can benefit from good management.

Given that there is a need for risk management, it is then natural to follow up by asking why a book specifically for nonprofit risk management. Admittedly, there are many excellent books that explain in detail the steps to great risk management. However, virtually all of them, with a few notable exceptions, focus on for-profit organizations. However, as we discuss in the following section there are several important distinctions between the for-profit firm and the nonprofit organization. For this reason, it is necessary to have a book that focuses on the specific needs of the nonprofit organization.

Nonprofits, by their very nature, tend to be very narrowly focused on a specific goal or objectives. While nonprofit organizations range in size, and some nonprofits are, indeed, quite large and even global in scope, the reality is that their missions tend to be quite focused compared to similarly sized corporations. As such, the method of doing things in nonprofits tends to be much more by default than in the wider-scaled for-profit corporation, which must explicitly consider risk management in order to manage its activities. The resulting lack of focus that many (if not most) nonprofits have on risk management means taking unnecessary risks, incurring unnecessary losses, and missing opportunities that a more robust attention to risk management may have avoided.

The final, and, perhaps, the most important reason for a book about risk management for nonprofits is that the risk management needs of nonprofits are unique.

What Is Different about Risk Management for Nonprofits?

The profit function of a corporation provides a focus, but it also gives an incentive for a corporation to spread out and diversify its activities. Nonprofits, by their nature, tend to remain much more focused. This implies that the nonprofit is more concentrated in their risks, which could be positive or negative.

The more concentrated risks of a nonprofit mean that the risk management function does generally not need to be as extensive or as comprehensive. Conversely, the lack of diversity means that the nonprofit can benefit more from risk management, as its more concentrated risks mean more concentrated and significant benefits from proper risk management.

The staffing of a nonprofit is also a factor to consider in designing the risk management plan. Many nonprofits operate with a largely volunteer board, and perhaps volunteer staff as well. In contrast, a corporation, particularly a publicly traded corporation, will have a diverse staff, with a variety of specialized skills, and a board and management team that are both diverse and individually highly specialized. The specializations of board members and management and volunteers of nonprofits tend to be in the area in which the mission of the organization is existent. They generally do not have the functional expertise in specific areas that are required. This is especially true in terms of risk management.

In terms of operations of a nonprofit, the passion and energy of staff and volunteers can make up for the lack of technical and functional expertise. This, however, is generally not the case for risk management. Exasperating the problem is that it is quite likely that the nonprofit team would recognize that they have a weakness in risk management expertise.

It is common knowledge that they need some skill in developing a strategic plan, a financial plan, and an operational plan, but it is much less common knowledge that a risk management plan is also part of a well-functioning and governed organization.

The issue of ignorance of managerial blind spots is often evident at the board level. While many nonprofits are very well managed and governed, it is also true that the board members of many nonprofits are chosen more for their connection with the cause of the organization than for their governance expertise. The classic example of this are the parents of children in a sporting organization. A typical board of a sports organization is made up of a collection of parents, coaches, and former athletes. The only common thread, and the only reason for selection, is the connection, past or present, with the sport itself. Little to no thought is given to the construction of the board in terms of function or managerial diversity. Although we have used a sports example, the same is also true of many nonprofit boards whether they be of a charity, a school-related cause, a health cause, or some other specific category. The common connection of the board members and volunteers (and frequently the staff) is their connection to the cause and little else. This connection can aid in furthering the cause but produces managerial holes in the day-to-day operations. It can also cause conflict as everyone may view the cause solely through their unique point of view.

The risk management function thus provides a common focal point for operations and decisions within the organization that may otherwise be missing. Thus, implementing risk management not only provides the benefits of risk management that exist in for-profit institutions but also provides extra benefits in terms of a focal point for the consistent management of the nonprofit organization.

Who May Benefit from This Book

This book is written for the stakeholders of the nonprofit organization. These stakeholders include managers, board members, regulators, and staff members. Ultimately, it is meant to be a guide for everyone involved in making and implementing decisions in a nonprofit.

Managers will benefit by learning techniques and tactics of understanding and managing risk. Board members will benefit from better understanding how strategic planning and risk planning are intertwined. Staff members will better appreciate how risk management can help them successfully complete tasks in a more efficient and effective way.

The book is written to be as accessible as possible. Wherever possible, nontechnical language is used. The intention is to write a book that can be a comprehensive source that can be widely and effectively used throughout the organization. The aim is to help nonprofits improve their operations through better risk management.

Ultimately, the book is written for everyone who has a stake in the long-term survival and success of the nonprofit organization.

Concluding Thoughts

We wrote this book for two fundamental reasons: we are passionate about risk management, and we are passionate about nonprofit organizations. It is our sincere hope that both of these passions have come through in this book and that this book serves, in at least some small way, a useful aid to those who choose to serve in nonprofits.

CHAPTER 1

What Is Risk? What Is Risk Management?

What Is Risk?

What is risk? It is such a simple and basic question. When we run risk workshops, we generally get started with this question and then are almost always surprised by the wide variety of answers provided. Some seminar participants give very sophisticated answers, while others give much more basic answers. It seems as if everyone has their own separate and distinct definition—even those that are from the same organization.

In the management literature, there are several different definitions of risk as well. They range from the highly technical or mathematical to the very basic. A common mathematical definition is that risk is the variance of results. A less technical definition is that risk is any event that causes deviations from an organization achieving its desired goals and objectives. Perhaps asking for the definition of risk is not so basic a question and worthy of a bit more analysis.

There is, however, one common element that people generally cite when asked for their definition of risk, and that is that risk is something to be avoided. They say things such as "risk is the possibility that something bad will happen" or "risk is the chance that you will lose" or "risk is danger." We believe that such negative definitions of risk are very limiting and hamper proper risk management.

Our definition of risk is "the possibility that bad or good things may happen." It may seem strange to include a positive element into the definition of risk, but it aligns with good risk practice, and it is also consistent with how risk is generally measured. It also makes it clear that the purpose of risk management is solely to aid the organization in implementing its strategy and achieving its objectives.

There are three distinct elements of our definition of risk. The first is an element of possibility. The second element is that risk is concerned with future events. Risk is looking backward only in order to learn from past experiences. Risk, however, is ultimately about future events. The third element is that risk can be positive or negative; that is, there is good risk, and there is bad risk. It is useful to take a moment and explore each of these three elements.

Risk is about not knowing what is going to happen. Risk is pregnant with possibility. Sometimes we can conjecture about what will happen, and sometimes we cannot. Sometimes risk is separated from uncertainty based on the types of possibilities. For instance, when I flip a coin in the air, I know that it can land either on heads or on tails. I know the possible outcomes, and I know the probabilities that it would land on heads is 50 percent; what I don't know is which of the two outcomes will occur and thus I have a risk. Conversely consider the occupations that will exist in 50 years from now. Just as 50 years ago we could not have conceived of a web developer or a mobile phone app programmer, the occupations of the future are unknown and at present inconceivable to us. We do not know what the possible outcomes are, nor do we know the associated probabilities.

The secretary of defense under George W. Bush, Donald Rumsfeld, famously stated his "unknown unknowns" quote:

> Reports that say that something hasn't happened are always interesting to me, because as we know, there are known knowns; there are things we know we know. We also know there are known unknowns; that is to say we know there are some things we do not know. But there are also unknown unknowns—the ones we don't know we don't know. And if one looks throughout the history of our country and other free countries, it is the latter category that tend to be the difficult ones.[1]

---

[1] https://en.wikipedia.org/wiki/There_are_known_knowns (accessed May 13, 2019).

The quote is so famous and well known that it even has its own Wikipedia page. The point is that in terms of risk management Donald Rumsfeld was onto something. There are risks that we know about, and risks that we do not know about. Proper risk management needs to be able to deal with and manage both types of risks. As pointed out by Rumsfeld, it is the unknown unknowns that tend to be the more difficult ones to deal with.

It may seem that we are belaboring this point, but our experience in risk management has taught us that the known risks tend to be the risks that are dealt with, but the more important and more valuable unknown unknowns risks tend to be ignored (either consciously or unconsciously) and thus risk management fails to be effective.

The second element of our definition is that risk is forward looking. In part, the forward nature of risk creates the uncertainty, and it is also the part that makes it difficult. Many organizations try to risk-manage the past, but that is mostly a fruitless exercise. "What's done is done" is a well-known expression along with "you cannot change the past." The past is only relevant for risk management to the extent that lessons can be learned and that those lessons will be relevant in the future. Ironically, however, risks, both positive and negative, tend to occur in an idiosyncratic manner with different outcomes and implications each time. In other words, the lessons of the past are often of little value for dealing with future risks. However, some risks do have a habit of reoccurring, and these "known knowns" can and should be dealt with by proper risk management.

The key point is that not even the best of risk management systems can do anything about the past. Risk management can, however, do something about the future—even if that future is uncertain. Thinking about risk is just like what you would typically do when driving a car; it is best done by looking through the front windshield rather than being overly occupied with what is happening in the rear-view mirror. That does not mean you ignore what you see in the rear-view mirror, particularly if it is relevant or a precursor to what is upcoming. It does imply, though, that eyes front should always be a priority.

The third element of our definition of risk is that risk has both positive and negative elements. Admittedly this is not always widely accepted, and it is not how many people view risk. However, there are several excellent reasons for considering risk this way. The first is that it implies that risk can be opportunistic. This, in turn, leads to risk management tactics being used not only to prevent unwelcome results but also to improve the number and size of unexpectedly good outcomes.

Another significant advantage of having a two-sided definition of risk is that it produces a more positive culture surrounding risk management. Instead of risk management being the "department of No!" it becomes the function of asking, "How can we do things more risk intelligently?" This is a theme that we will repeatedly return to and one that makes risk management an asset to the organization rather than a drag and a cost. It may be a subtle change in the outlook on risk, but it makes a significant difference in the effectiveness of risk management.

What Is Risk Management?

If risk is the possibility that bad or good things may happen, that thus makes risk management the function of managing so as to increase the probability and magnitude of occurrence of good risk while simultaneously managing so as to decrease the probability and severity of occurrence of bad risk.

Risk management is a proactive activity for managing both upside and downside risk. Risk management is as much about preventing unwanted outcomes as it is about being in position to capitalize on opportunities. Negative events are simply the flip side of positive outcomes. The same activities that are used to prevent negative risks can be used to seize upon positive risks.

Being proactive means that risk management is both an active and ongoing set of activities as well as a planned set of activities. Too often, risk management is thought of as a set of actions that are taken after something has happened. In such situations, risk management becomes crisis management. In our opinion, crisis management is what needs to be done only if risk management is not an active part of an organization's activities. Crisis management is separate from risk management, and a separate crisis management plan should be in place. Likely the crisis management plan will be informed by the risk management plan and activities, but the two are not substitutes for each other.

As the preceding brief discussion of crisis management highlights, it is important to be clear about not only what risk management is but also what it is not. First and foremost, risk management is not compliance management. While compliance management is important, it needs to be realized that compliance management is set to achieve the objectives of the regulators of the organization. While the objectives of the regulators may be in line with the strategic objectives of the organization, it is not a given and, indeed, is often a poor assumption. How many times have you heard an organization say that they were not responsible for avoiding a preventable debacle since they followed all of the regulations? Additionally, an organization is likely to have additional goals and objectives that go well beyond those of the regulators. As discussed in the following section, risk management should be in line with the goals and objectives of an organization.

We suggest that organizations keep regulatory compliance as a necessary but not sufficient part of risk management. The risk management function and tactics would ideally capture whatever synergies are possible with compliance management. However, when these synergies are not present, a separate set of risk management guidelines, metrics, and procedures should be put in place.

An additional concept to remember is that the regulators will not understand or know the functioning of an organization as well as the managers and the board of the organization. Regulators by necessity are forced to create a broad set of guidelines that may or may not pertain to the specifics of each and every organization. Thus, an organization should be sure to create and implement a risk management plan that is specifically suited to their own context. An additional component of compliance is that it is often based almost exclusively on the past, with limited attention paid to the future or planned changes in the activities of the organization. Thus, the future-looking nature of risk management implies that while compliance is necessary, it is not sufficient for risk management.

Additionally, a risk management plan is not a control mechanism. While controls will likely be part of risk management activities, according to author and enterprise risk management consultant James Lam, the objective is to operate in a "control environment, not an environment of control."[2]

---

[2]J. Lam. 2014. *Enterprise Risk Management: From Incentives to Controls* (2nd ed.; Hoboken, NJ: Wiley).

If a conscious effort is made in managing both upside and downside risk, the outcome will be that risk management activities become an enabler for an organization. It changes the risk management function from one of being "the department of No!" to "the department of how to do it more risk intelligently." This subtle change in focus can completely change the attitude toward risk management in an organization and create a more helpful and healthier risk culture.

Risk Management as a Strategic Activity

A central tenet of risk management is that it is a core part of strategic management and objective management. Ultimately risk management is an activity to help an organization reach its strategic goals and objectives. If risk management is not doing that, then, at best, it is compliance activity. As discussed in both Chapters 3 and 11 ("Risk Management Frameworks" and "Risk Governance," respectively), the risk management activities of a firm should be explicitly aligned with their strategic objectives. It is only by doing this that risk management becomes a value-added activity rather than a cost center.

As a strategic activity, risk management must also be tied to the operational realities of an organization. There is a right amount of risk management. Too much risk management and it becomes an unnecessarily bulky, clunky, and superfluous set of activities. Too little risk management and the organization is exposed to downside risks and will likely miss upside opportunities or be unable to capitalize on them.

The development of the risk management plan and the strategic plan of an organization is an exercise that is ideally done in tandem. The risk management knowledge provides input to the development of the strategic plan. In turn, the strategic plan drives risk management activities. Both plans inform, guide, and support each other.

In a well-functioning organization, with a mature and robust risk management structure, strategic planning and risk management are virtually one and the same. A specific case in point is the situation of Hydro One. Hydro One is the power distribution utility for the province of Ontario, Canada. As outlined in an extensive case study, the risk management plan was explicitly tied to the development of the strategic plan.[3] Capital was allocated based on needs to manage risk, and thus essentially the operations of the utility were indistinguishable from the risk management operations. As a consequence, the role of the chief risk officer became almost superfluous. Risk management became indistinguishable from management, and Hydro One became a model of risk management.

Risk Management as a Value-Added Activity

Risk management should be both an enabler of the organization and a value-added activity. Risk management activities should enable a nonprofit to more effectively and efficiently carry out its strategic plan and provide the goods and services that it has as its mission. Depending on the scope and scale of a risk management process needed, the development of a risk management process can be lengthy and costly in terms of time, energy, and resources. However, there are many benefits from implementing risk management such that the overall return from risk management activities should be strongly positive.

The first and primary benefit of implementing risk management is that it increases the possibility of good outcomes, while simultaneously it also reduces the probability and severity of negative outcomes. This is the primary function of risk management, and it is thus also the primary benefit. Again, it is important to realize the two-way benefit: not only avoiding negative surprises but also being better positioned to take advantage of positive surprises or uncertainty.

A widely cited standard for enterprise risk management is the Committee of Sponsoring Organizations of the Treadway Commission, which is better known as COSO. Although the COSO risk management framework is designed for for-profit organizations, there are six frequently cited advantages associated with adopting the COSO risk framework that are also applicable to nonprofit organizations. These six advantages of adopting risk management as stated by COSO are "(1) Increase the range of

---

[3]T. Aabo, J.R.S. Fraser, and B.J. Simkins. 2005. "The Rise and Evolution of the Chief Risk Officer: Enterprise Risk Management at Hydro One," *Journal of Applied Corporate Finance* 17, no. 3, pp. 62-75.

opportunities, (2) Identify and manage entity-wide risks, (3) Increasing positive outcomes and advantage while reducing negative surprises, (4) Reduce performance variability, (5) Improve resource deployment, and (6) Enhancing enterprise resilience."[4]

These six benefits are obviously applicable to both for-profit and nonprofit organizations. Additionally, there are more benefits that accrue to nonprofits. One key additional benefit is a better understanding of the organization. Implementing and carrying out the steps of a risk management strategy and plan increases the knowledge of the opportunities and hazards of managing the organization. This is key for a nonprofit of whom many operators and directors may be part-time employees or volunteers. Their knowledge of the organization, and of organizational practices, may be limited, as their association with the organization is limited. A risk plan helps to get everyone knowledgeable with the organization's operations and possibilities. This, in turn, leads to not only better understanding and better management but also enhanced engagement. This enhanced engagement can occur at the board level as well as at the grassroots volunteer level. This is critical especially for those who are part-time employees or volunteers who have conflicted demands on their time and energy. An engaged base is a unique problem for nonprofits, as staff generally do not have the same financial incentives as they do in for-profit organizations. Thus, enhanced engagement and understanding that is aided or facilitated by risk management structure can be a significant value-added benefit of risk management.

Proper adoption of risk management will also increase discipline in planning and in the implementation of operational tactics. The forward-looking nature of risk management increases the focus on the future and thus improves strategic planning, which should also be a forward-looking exercise. As part of the planning process, the metrics developed through risk management will likely prove to be a valuable asset in improving strategic and operational plans.

Ultimately the close linkage between risk management and strategic management implies that the better the risk management of an

---

[4]https://www.coso.org/Documents/2017-COSO-ERM-Integrating-with-Strategy-and-Performance-Executive-Summary.pdf (accessed May 14, 2019).

organization, the better the management of an organization. This enhanced management has value of its own beyond the obvious. Better management as facilitated by risk management can enhance the reputation of a nonprofit firm, and in doing so give volunteers, patrons, and other stakeholders more confidence and more willingness in assisting the nonprofit in achieving its objectives. Overall, risk management can be a complete win for the wide variety of stakeholders that play a role in the organization.

Basic Steps of Risk Management

In the rest of the book we go through the steps of risk management. At this introductory point, however, it is useful to say a few words about a few of the big picture themes in setting up risk management. We have already discussed the importance of aligning risk management with the strategic objectives. However, it is useful to ask what an organization hopes to achieve by implementing risk management.

The previous section has given a lengthy list of benefits of adopting risk management. It is useful to be specific, though, about the benefits that it is hoped to achieve. A knowledge of why a firm is adopting risk management—beyond the vague "it will make us a better organization"— is useful in helping to direct the development and implementation of risk management.

Risk management is a process, and without an idea of the main hoped-for outcomes, the development of effective risk management is likely to take much longer time than what is necessary. Lacking a clear goal for the "why" of risk management has anecdotally been a major reason why so many implementations of risk management processes have been so costly or so ineffective in the for-profit world. Many for-profit organizations have started on risk management implementations without a clear goal of what they hoped to achieve. Many started implementing a risk management protocol simply to keep up with others in the same industry who had done so. They wanted to reap the benefits without really understanding what benefits of risk management were most important to them.

At a conference once, one of the authors was told by a conference presenter (who was a senior risk manager in a for-profit company) that one should expect risk management implementation to take four times longer time than the worst estimates and to cost four times more than the worst estimates. When asked why their corporation bothered to implement risk management in the first place, the presenter had no idea. Don't let that example be your guide for risk management implementation.

The basic steps of risk management can be broken down into three basic questions: (1) Where are we now? (2) Where do we want to be? and (3) How are we going to get there?

Asking, "Where are we now?" is asking what we currently do in terms of risk management. How well does the organization understand the threats and opportunities that it has before it? How well is the organization positioned to manage these threats and to take advantage of the opportunities?

A useful risk exercise is to look forward 5 years or perhaps 10 years depending on the nature of the environment for the organization and speculate that the organization has missed achieving its goals and objectives. (Note: this miss could be underperformance or overperformance relative to the objectives.) Given the hypothetical assumption that the organization has missed its objectives, how comfortable are you that you know the reasons why it missed achieving those objectives? The level of comfort with the answer to this speculative exercise is directly related to where the organization is in risk management. A high level of comfort implies that the organization comfortably understands its risks. A low level of comfort implies that the organization has some development of its risk knowledge and understanding to do. The second part of this thought exercise is to ask if the organization knows about how to increase the probability of achieving its objectives and if it has in place a plan to implement those actions.

The preceding thought exercise is a very powerful one. However, it is very difficult to do without an outside facilitator. The members who are most involved in an organization are frequently blinded to threats and opportunities by their familiarity with the organization, and this is true in for-profit as well as nonprofit organizations. Additionally, they may be biased based on their belief in the mission of the organization. It has been our experience that nonprofit workers and volunteers tend to be very well intended but are heavily influenced by their connection. They likely do not see the threats and opportunities in the same way that an outsider would.

The second question is, "Where do we want to be?" This is a difficult question for many organizations to answer, as they may not be familiar with the possibilities that an effective risk management plan may bring. This is where benchmarking to other nonprofit organizations that have implemented risk management practices comes into play. The benefits of risk management have been listed previously, but it is often only through viewing another similar organization's success with risk management that the benefits can be truly appreciated.

Answering the question, "Where do we want to be?" is both a strategic question and a practical operational question. Recall the discussion on the right amount of risk management. Too much risk management can be as ineffective and as inefficient as too little risk management. It is best to be realistic in both time and scope when answering this question. As with any major initiative, too much, implemented too quickly, can be both ineffective and demoralizing.

The final step is to answer the question, "How do we get there?" This is the basic operational question of risk management and the focus of the rest of the book. For now, the how-do-we-get-there can be broken down into some basic steps that are common to all risk frameworks. The first step is setting the objective for risk management, which should be aligned with the strategy of the organization and being aware of the context of the stakeholders of the organization. The next step is to identify the risks and analyze those risks in terms of their probabilities of occurring, potential impact if they do occur, and the amount of control that may be possible over those risks for the organization. What follows next is a decision to be made about how each of the risks is to be treated or managed. In conjunction with this is designing a series of methods to measure and communicate the risks throughout the organization and to the relevant stakeholders. Additionally how to measure the effectiveness of the risk management itself and how it might be improved on a continuous basis need to be thought of.

The exact steps for implementing risk management should be specific and tailored for each organization. The aforementioned is meant as a broad guideline. A more detailed discussion of risk frameworks will be presented in Chapter 3.

Complexity Science and Risk

Before finishing this chapter, it is worthwhile to take a moment to mention an evolving field of thought in risk management that concerns the discipline of complexity science and its associated phenomenon of emergence.

Whenever a group of agents (in the context of nonprofits, think of the various stakeholders of the organization) can interact (e.g., through face-to-face interactions, the media, or social media) and can adapt (change their opinions or change their actions), then the potential for complexity arises. Complexity is a phenomenon that we observe in mobs, in bumble bees, in climate change, in economic booms and busts, and a wide variety of other fields and applications.[5]

"Complex" and "complicated" are frequently used as synonyms by lay people. To scientists who study systems, such as social systems, complex systems and complicated systems are very different types of systems. Complicated systems are those that operate by well-known rules or laws, such as the laws of physics or mathematics. Conversely, complex systems have no such rules. While there may be social customs, there is no rule that states how you greet a coworker first thing in the morning; it could be with a big smile and a "what a beautiful morning," or it could be with a weary "how ya doing—another day at the grind." However, the laws of physics state, and repeatedly reinforce, that if you let go of your coffee mug midair, it will always fall to the floor and not suspend itself midair.[6]

A key implication of complexity is emergence. Emergence is when patterns of action between the agents become significant and visible. For instance, a murmuration of starlings,[7] or the pooling of a school of fish, or the way that certain consumer fads such as fidget spinners or pet rocks

---

[5]For an introduction to complexity, see F. Westley, B. Zimmerman, and M.Q. Patton. 2006. *Getting to Maybe: How the World is Changed* (Toronto, Canada: Random House).

[6]For an introduction to the difference between complicated and complexity, see R. Nason. 2017. *It's Not Complicated: The Art and Science of Complexity in Business* (Toronto, Canada: University of Toronto Press).

[7]If you are not familiar with a murmuration of starlings, do a search of the Internet for a video. It is a dramatic and impressive thing to observe and is a perfect illustration of complexity and emergence.

become extremely popular but just as fast peter out are all examples of emergence. Emergence trends are extremely important in social sciences and are becoming recognized for their importance in risk management as well.

Complicated systems are completely predictable. They are also reducible. The classic example of a complicated system is a fine Swiss-made watch. It operates on springs and gears, each of which is subject to the physics of springs and the mathematics of gears. If a watch is not working properly, you can disassemble the watch, repair the malfunctioning part, reassemble the watch, and it will work again, just like when it was new.

Complex systems, however, are not predictable. Additionally, they are not reducible. Take for instance the rise in popularity of a music star. There are no rules or laws for becoming a best-selling musician. While you need talent, it is not necessarily the most talented that rise to the top. You also need charisma; but what defines charisma, and how do you replicate it? When a music star has their fame start to dim, you cannot fix the fame as you do a watch. There is not one specific thing that you can label that causes them to lose their fame.

Complex problems are important for risk management, as many significant risk issues arise from complex situations. This is particularly true for a nonprofit firm that generally has a wide variety of different agents (volunteers, staff, beneficiaries, benefactors, governmental agencies), all of whom have different goals and interests, and all of whom will interact with each other in different ways and with different worldviews and assumptions. The difficulty for risk management is that complicated problems can be solved, while complex problems, at best, must be managed. There is no magic formula that solves complex situations.

There are three main considerations when dealing with complex situations as a risk manager. The first is to recognize the type of system that a given situation falls under. Is the situation a complex one, or is it complicated? If it is complicated, then figure out the rules to fix it. The second step is to realize that complex problems, at best, can be managed, but they cannot be solved. Related to this is the third consideration that complex systems require you to adopt a "try, learn, adapt" approach. You cannot be dogmatic in dealing with complex risk; the best you can do is to try something, learn from what the outcomes are, and adapt or adjust your approach as best as you can.[8]

Complexity admittedly makes the job of risk management seem much more difficult. It would be relatively easy, and indeed, conceptually it would be possible to optimize risk management if only all risks were complicated. If all risks were complicated, then a master risk formula would be written and an optimum risk plan created. The risk plan would be implemented and managed by a bot or a master computer algorithm that follows the rules that govern the complicated risks.

The reality is that many of the most significant risks are complex, or a combination of complex and complicated parts. Complexity is a reality, and the organization that ignores this fact is not only fooling itself but also setting itself up to have an ineffective strategy and an ineffective risk plan. Furthermore, not only will the risk plan be ineffective, but it will be frustratingly so.

Complexity management will be mentioned at various places throughout this book. Complexity is particularly significant when it comes to dealing with people risk and reputational risk. Ultimately, the best management tool for complex risk management is to build a risk culture that is robust yet resilient and flexible.

Risk Management Is an Active, Not a Passive Activity

Often, risk management is thought of as a "put in place and forget it" type of management action. We believe that this is a serious mistake for a variety of reasons. The first and immediate reason is that complexity means that risks tend to evolve, or more technically risks tend to exhibit emergence.

As the future is not static, risks are not static. Although nonprofits generally do not have to compete like for-profit corporations do (the big exception possibly being competing for funding from sponsors), the environment in which nonprofits operate is, nonetheless, dynamic. The needs of beneficiaries change, the technologies and the mode to serve

---

[8]A more detailed discussion in managing complex risk situations in R. Nason. 2018. *Rethinking Risk Management: Critically Examining Old Ideas and New Concepts* (New York, NY: Business Expert Press).

beneficiaries change, staffing changes, and the demands and desires of sponsors change. These dynamics change the risks and thus change how the risk management plan should be designed and implemented.

The active dynamic of risk also requires a risk manager to be creative. This creativity extends to the identification of risk through to the management of risk. The first law of risk management is that the mere fact that you identify that a risk exists automatically implies that your management of it will improve. The complexity of risk, the dynamic nature of risk, and the uncertainty inherent in risk all require the risk manager and the risk management system to be creative, flexible, and resilient.

Concluding Thoughts

This introductory chapter has introduced the basics of risk and risk management, and in particular why a nonprofit organization needs to be concerned about risk.

There are numerous advantages for a nonprofit to take risk management seriously and integrate it into the strategic planning and operations of the organization. However, to receive the full amount of the benefits, it is important that risk management be seen as managing both the upside opportunities and the downside negatives. Appreciating that risk is the possibility that bad or good things may happen allows for a much higher value-added outcome of the risk management function.

Three basic questions cover the overview of starting a risk management program: (1) Where are we now? (2) Where do we want to be? and (3) How are we going to get there? These three questions could have just as easily been asked at a strategic planning meeting. This is not a coincidence, as strategic planning and risk planning in our view are two sides of the same coin. Risk management and strategic management are two closely intertwined activities that inform and complement each other.

This chapter has also introduced the concept of complexity, which may be new to many readers. Complexity has many implications for risk management. As will be discussed throughout this book, some of the more impactful risks are those that are complex. Complexity implies that risk management is both a creative and an ongoing activity, one that requires thoughtful, aware, and active management.

CHAPTER 2

Basic Principles of Risk

In this chapter we present some general principles for good risk management and dispel some common myths. The first, and in our opinion, most important principle of risk management is getting a proper understanding of what risk is and what risk management is. This, of course, has been covered in the previous chapter. The overarching principle of risk as the possibility of occurrence of good or bad things is key. Furthermore, understanding that risk managing is acting so as to increase the probability and magnitude of occurrence of good things while decreasing the probability and magnitude of occurrence of bad things is also essential. With that understanding in hand, the rest is relatively straightforward common sense. However, a variety of agents, ranging from consultants to regulators to well-meaning benefactors, sometimes manage to make risk management seem like an overly onerous and difficult task. In this chapter we reinforce some common-sense principles, but first we start with challenging some common myths about risk and risk management.

Some Common Risk Management Myths

The first and perhaps most perverse myth about risk management is that it is a science. Nothing could be further from the truth. Risk management is about managing the unexpected and the uncertain. Science is about knowing the certain and the expected. Consequently, risk and science are almost exact opposites of each other. Additionally, there are two other components that prevent risk management from being a science: complexity and accidents.

In Chapter 1, we have discussed the role that complexity plays in risk management. In later chapters, there will be numerous examples where complexity again arises as a central feature. Complexity management is not scientific management in the way that the term is generally understood. Scientific management is based on finding an optimal solution with a known outcome, while in complexity management, the best available solution produces an outcome of "maybe."

Accidents are also a part of risk management. Accidents, both happy accidents and unfortunate accidents, occur. Risk management is about being ready for and able to accept or capitalize upon the accidents. Science does not readily admit to the existence of accidents. Nor does it admit to human error, lapses in judgment, or irrational behavior—all important factors in risk and risk management.

If the world were completely knowable and forecastable, and if nonprofits operated as if they were subjected to a set of scientific laws and irrefutable mathematical relationships like a fine Swiss watch, then we would not need risk management. In such an idealistic world, nonprofits, and all organizations for that matter, would be run by a giant computer that would produce optimized inputs and outputs. The reality is that nonprofits operate in the much messier world of people and their diverse desires, abilities, and needs.

Related to the science myth of risk management, there is the myth that risk management is all about the mathematics of risk. Indeed, there are a few specialty areas of risk management that do involve a lot of mathematics; however, that is not the case for most areas of risk, and it is definitely not so for nonprofits. As will be discussed at length later in this chapter, risk is fundamentally about people and their interactions. People do not submit to the whims of a mathematical algorithm or theory. This is, in part, what makes risk management such an interesting field.

Looking at risk management outside of the realm of nonprofits, it can be argued that the financial collapse of 2008 was precipitated by a critical mass of institutions and regulators believing that risk management could be managed and controlled through the use of scientific principles and the rigors of mathematical relationships. That line of thinking failed badly for financial institutions, and we believe that a strict adherence to believing that risk is based on science and mathematics will end just as suboptimally for nonprofit organizations.

Auditing is another discipline that is often commingled with risk management. Auditing is making sure that procedures are being following and that the data is correct. While auditing can play a central role in effective risk management, it is not a replacement for risk management. Just because an organization passes an audit, it does not mean that it is operating its risk management in an optimal manner.

Auditing as a risk management substitute fails for two major reasons. The first is that while auditing does the important task of checking that processes have been followed and that the recorded information is correct, the reality is that the more important task is to determine what the right processes are, how those processes are changing, and what new processes need to be added, and which ones are no longer necessary. Likewise, knowing that the numbers are correct is meaningless if they are not the numbers that are needed for effective risk management. Risk management is an active thinking task, while auditing is a passive task. Auditing is like a university teaching assistant, while risk management is like a university professor. The teaching assistant does the important task of marking the exams and assignments, but the professor is the one who determines the proper questions to ask on the exams and assignments. Auditing does the checking, but risk management sets the questions that need to be checked. Both tasks are necessary, but one alone is not a sufficient substitute for the other.

For similar reasons as auditing, compliance also fails as a method of risk management. Compliance has an additional flaw as a risk management technique, that is, compliance is set by the regulators. Regulators have their own goals and objectives, which most likely are not aligned with the goals and objectives of an organization. Furthermore, the regulators are generally much more concerned about downside risk than they are about upside risk. This misalignment means that compliance will not be an effective substitute for risk management.

Obviously, an organization needs compliance and needs to observe and obey all relevant regulations. We are not saying that compliance is bad, but we are stating that the differing objectives between regulators and organizations need to be acknowledged. Organizations that strive to be most effective in their risk management will obviously stay in compliance, and do all of the tasks that compliance requires, but they will keep a separate set of metrics, procedures, and tactics that they do that are over and above the compliance regulations.

Finally, we come to processes. Many organizations believe that a rigid and comprehensive set of processes is sufficient for effective risk management. Again, we believe that reality is a bit more nuanced. Processes are very important for risk management, but again, they are not sufficient. Processes need to be balanced with judgment. However, it is very difficult to know when to rely on a process or when to shift and go with one's judgment. The question is compounded by the fact that many nonprofits are staffed by volunteers, who may or may not have the experience or expertise, nor the institutional knowledge that is necessary to be able to rely on one's judgment.

Having processes as a major risk management tactic has many advantages. Processes can be developed using knowledge and experience of experts. In this way best practice can be incorporated. Processes are also developed in advance, and proactivity is almost always a great practice to follow for risk management. Finally, processes allow for consistency in best practice, which is key, particularly when an organization's functions are carried out by volunteers who may have limited knowledge or experience.

There are, however, several problems with processes as a major risk management tool. To begin with, major risk events are almost always about exceptional circumstances. Processes are great for managing the normal, high-frequency but general, low-impact day-to-day risks. When the situation is unusual, or idiosyncratic, and has the potential for high impact, processes may hinder rather than help risk management.

A classic case study for this is that of Tomas Lopez. Tomas was a lifeguard in the city of Hallandale Beach, Florida. As a lifeguard, Tomas had the important risk management task of making sure that people at the beach were safe, and he was suitably trained and certified to save them if they got into distress. As part of the process for being a lifeguard, it was clearly stated that if someone was in distress outside of the designated swimming area, the lifeguards were to call for outside emergency help (essentially dial 911) and simply wait for the external help to arrive. This policy is sound and has a lot of best practice to support it. First, one should not put at risk the people who are following the rules and staying within the designated swimming areas by attending to those who are flouting the rules. Second, it ensures that lifeguard resources are not spread too thinly. Third, it encourages people to follow the reasonable rules of enjoying the beach safely. The policy of not actively going to save swimmers in distress outside of the designated and roped-off area is a sound one and a practice that is in place at most supervised beaches.

Human nature being what it is, it so happened that on a day that Tomas was working, a swimmer got into distress outside of the designated area. What Tomas and his employers did then made national headlines. Tomas quickly summoned other lifeguards to cover for him, as he went to rescue the person in distress outside of the designated area. The person was saved by Tomas's quick action, but Tomas was subsequently fired for not following the process.

Putting aside the moral and ethical implications of Tomas's actions, what action would you have wanted Tomas to take? Obviously if you were the swimmer in distress, you would want him to save you. The issue is more complicated if you are the manager of the lifeguards. What would be the implications if, while Tomas was saving the rogue swimmer in distress, someone within the designated swimming area also suffered distress and subsequently died due to the lack of lifeguards as Tomas was occupied? What are the implications as observers see that the lifeguards routinely rescue people outside the designated area; will this lead to a larger number of people ignoring common-sense beach safety rules? Will the subsequent media attention paid to Tomas Lopez and his situation lead to the lifeguards performing ever more heroic actions, putting both themselves and the swimmers at increasing levels of danger as they too seek their moments of fame? If one rule for the lifeguards can be broken, does this imply that other rules for the lifeguards can also be broken?

The process versus judgment debate is an extensive one among risk management professionals. The important point to take away is that processes have significant advantages to offer to risk management, but they do not necessarily comprise a complete risk management strategy by themselves. There will always be room for judgment.

Finally, there is the myth that risk management eliminates mistakes, mishaps, and even risk itself. During the financial crisis of 2008, financial firms and regulators were blamed for their poor risk management. The basis for these claims was that if effective risk management was in place that the financial collapse would not have occurred. That is an inaccurate way to think about risk management. All of the major institutions involved had state-of-the-art risk management in place and the best of risk management thinking guiding their actions. In fact, the problem may have been too much risk management![1]

You may recall that in Chapter 1 we stated that risk management was managing so as to increase the probability and magnitude of occurrence of good risk events while also decreasing the probability and magnitude of occurrence of bad risk events. There will always be probabilities and uncertainties associated with risk management. There is an old saying in risk management that the only perfect hedge is in a Japanese garden. No risk management technique is perfect, nor should it be. Every risk management action involves trade-offs and compromises.

Furthermore, organizations should not strive to eliminate risk. Organizations are in place in order to take risk. That is how they provide a service to their beneficiaries. In fact, some risks should be embraced and leveraged.

Risk management does not exist to eliminate risk. Risk management is to change both the probability and the size of the effect of risk. Risk management is about making active decisions on how to handle risk both proactively and in the moment. Risks are going to occur, no matter how extensive the risk management effort is. All risk cannot be eliminated, but risk outcomes can be improved.

Some Risk Management Truths

Risk management is about people. Risk is about people doing things, people interacting, and people creating. Risk management is about people's perceptions, biases, knowledge, beliefs, values, and competencies.

---

[1]Too much risk is a phenomenon known as risk homeostasis. Basically, risk homeostasis is when people feel extra safe when there are strong risk or safety barriers in place and thus undertake risky actions that they otherwise would not do without the risk measures. Interested readers may wish to refer to R. Nason. October, 2009. "Is Your Risk System Too Good?" *The RMA Journal* 2, no. 2, pp 12-15, 11.

Risk is about hope and fears, needs and desires. Risk is about people and all of their wonderful diversity.

Ultimately, risk management is people management. There are times when inanimate objects are the cause of risk, such as equipment failure, but these instances tend to be relatively minor. In any case, inanimate risk can also generally be relatively accurately calculated and prepared for. As artificial intelligence increases in importance and prevalence, the differences about risk as being people centric are likely to increase.

An interesting risk experiment is developing real time as self-driving automobiles become a reality. Self-driving automobiles are changing people's opinion not only about artificial intelligence but also about creating a new realization about the role that people, as opposed to machines, play in risk management. It is also exposing the fact that risk management cannot be simply reduced to the science and mathematics of risk. However, artificial intelligence as illustrated by self-driving cars has the potential to revolutionize risk management, as it is such a visible daily example of where AI and risk management meet.[2]

Self-driving automobiles are considered by many to have the potential to dramatically reduce automobile accidents. Not only will artificial intelligence create safer driving conditions, but it will also likely make driving much more efficient by dramatically reducing traffic jams as well as pollution from inefficient driving habits. Despite these efficiencies, though, there is a general public backlash against self-driving cars. Many people state that they will not feel safe with self-driving automobiles and that regulators are drawing up legislation to closely control them. When a self-driving automobile gets into an accident, it is national news, whereas auto accidents caused by humans are barely registered in the local news. In part, this is due to the novelty of self-driving automobiles, but it has also been suggested that it is because the public has a schadenfreude about the vehicles. Since we don't trust them, we relish the opportunity when we have an objective reason to criticize them. It is still early days for the industry, and the statistics could change with time and experience, but so far, the safety record of self-driving automobiles seems exemplary, yet we as a whole remain suspicious.

---

[2]We will have more to say about the role of artificial intelligence in risk management in Chapter 12, "The Future of Risk Management."

The experience with self-driving automobiles and artificial intelligence illustrates that at a root level, humans do not trust artificial intelligence. By extension, we can infer that humans will not trust artificial intelligence for risk management. Despite rationally knowing that many aspects of risk management are better done by bots and artificial intelligence, we still, irrationally, prefer to have a human at the controls.

If you are of a certain age, you will recall the introduction of automated teller machines (or ATMs). Probably the first time you used an ATM you were hesitant, insisted on getting a receipt, and you likely closely checked the receipt and even more closely checked the amount of money that the machine dispensed to you. It likely took you a while to get totally comfortable with using an ATM, but eventually you did. It is the same with risk management. It will take a while for us to get comfortable with AI controlling many aspects of our risk management.

It is important to note at this point that AI can only handle risks that are well defined and complicated in nature. AI cannot manage complex risks. Thus, the fact that we as humans do not trust AI, and that AI cannot manage complex risks, means that people will be a central part of risk management for a long time to come.

So we return to the fact that risk management could rightly be labeled people management. People are the root cause of the vast majority of significant risks, people are the ones who can manage risks, and people are the reason that nonprofits operate.

The realization that risk management is about people means that risk management should be designed for people. The design of risk management, and the development of the risk culture of the organization are key elements for successful risk management.

Design is an important component of risk management. Design not only leads to efficiencies in risk management but also leads to better adoption of risk management by the stakeholders of an organization. If risk management is designed for those who need to implement it, then the acceptance will be better, and implementation will be more than likely carried out as intended. If, however, the design of risk management is done without human consideration, then both its adoption and implementation efficiency will be seriously impaired.

As an example, remember the early design of seatbelts. They were uncomfortable, considered to be ugly, and rather clumsy. Acceptance of seatbelts was slow, and even when safety systems, such as warning bells, were installed to enforce its use, drivers found workarounds, such as keeping the belts constantly fastened but tucked into the seats where they could not be seen or felt. It was only when seatbelts were more integrated into the car design in a way that made them easy and comfortable to use that drivers began to readily accept them. Now, most drivers would not think of being in a car without them.

As humans are at the heart of risk management, the design of risk management should also be focused on the humans that the risk management technique is designed to serve and to be implemented by. As an aside, the design element is another reason that regulations that ignore design are not sufficient for effective risk management.

Risk management, due to the future being uncertain, is also about probabilities. A good risk manager understands probabilities. Note that such understanding may be at an intuitive level rather than the high school statistics class level. As previously emphasized, you do not need to be a mathematician to be a good risk manager, but you should have an intuitive feel for probabilities.

It is important to realize that probabilities are not certainties. We are sure that you know someone who grumbles when the weather forecaster says that there is only a 20 percent chance of showers, and then when it does rain, they claim that the forecaster is a no-good fraud. Related to this fallacy is mistaking a high probability as a certainty and a low probability as a certainty that an event would not happen. A high or low probability does not determine whether or not an event would occur.

People, in general, are not very good at understanding statistics and probability. There is an entire field of risk psychology that deals with how our biases and cognitive abilities blind us to the true level of risks that we are taking. Even professors of statistics and probability are prone to errors in interpreting perceived risk levels.

One issue with probability in risk management is the issue of frequentist statistics. Consider two simple coin-tossing games. In one game, the coin will be tossed once. If it comes up heads, you win $1,100,000. If it comes up tails, you lose $1,000,000. The expected value of this game is

$50,000. However, few people would choose to play this coin-flipping game in real life. The downside is simply too great, even given the positive expected outcome. While winning $1,100,000 would be fantastic, the consequences of losing would likely bankrupt most people.

Now consider a similar coin-tossing game. In this second game, a head means that you will win $1,100,000 and a tail means that you will lose $1,000,000 as before. In this game, however, the game will be played 1,000 times, and the net payment of winnings or losings will be made at the end of the 1,000 tosses. In this version of the game, the expected pay-out of each toss of the coin is the same, but the fact that it will be tossed 1,000 times totally changes your willingness to play. The probability of being a net loser is infinitesimally small, while the probability of winning a large sum is very high.

This coin-tossing example illustrates the issue of frequentist statistics. When it comes to risk management, we generally only get to make significant decisions once or twice. Our real-life decision making is analogous to playing the one-time coin-tossing game. In such situations our decision making cannot be made on a solely rational basis on the calculated probabilities.

Probability would be much more prominent in risk management, and in life, if only we had the opportunity to always hit the rest button on our decisions for such a number of trials so that the mathematically expected outcome became the realized outcome. That, however, is a fantasy world and we need to make decisions for the actual world that we live in. Thus, although probability is a guide in risk management, one must keep the realities of the issue of frequentist statistics in mind.

Another key component of good risk management centers on information and the communication of that information to the appropriate stakeholders. Coupled with information is the associated learning. Risk management is getting information—which sometimes you need to be creative about doing so—and using that information to make better risk decisions. Communicating that information throughout allows others in the organization to also make better decisions. Increasing the frequency of better risk decisions is ultimately what risk management is about.

Many organizations have extensive record keeping of their risks, frequently called a risk register. That is well and good, but it is what you do with that information that matters. Is that information widely disseminated? Is it used for learning? Is it used to develop better risk management techniques? Institutional knowledge is key in all areas, but especially so in risk management. We all know the adage that those who ignore the lessons of history are doomed to repeat their past mistakes.

Information is to be shared and used. It is to be shared with the relevant stakeholders and shared so that others may benefit from the gained knowledge.

Balancing the information is that risk is about uncertainty. There needs to be a realization that knowledge is constantly changing and thus will not always be consistently relevant. Coming back to the Donald Rumsfeld quote that was presented in the previous chapter, it is very true that risk management is about the "known knowns, the known unknowns and the unknown unknowns." While information helps us make better risk decisions, the reality is that it is simply not practical or sometimes even possible to know all the information that we need, much less gather and understand that information. Risk managers frequently have to make risk decisions based on incomplete or even incorrect information. Ironically, it is perhaps the easiest but most insignificant risk decisions are based on the known knowns, while the more significant and more challenging risk decisions are those that involve the unknown unknowns.

Given the variability in information and in the knowledge about the future, the risk manager must be creative. Creativity is key in uncovering potential risk issues, particularly in light of the first law of risk management (the mere fact that you acknowledge that a risk may exist automatically improves your management of it). Being creative in the creation of scenarios about what might go wrong or right in the achievement of the organization's goals certainly helps to develop better risk plans and strategies.

Creativity is also key to the development and implementation of risk strategies. The realities of complex risks are that what worked last time is not certain to work the next time a similar situation arises. Risks as they evolve tend to develop unique characteristics, so risk managers must be continually developing creative solutions.

Risk is a learning activity. It involves organizational learning, where the organization as a whole develops knowledge and intuition about how best to manage risk, but it also involves individual learning about risk tools, tactics, and strategies for the more effective management of risk.

Risk and the Connection with Strategy and Mission

The ultimate truth about risk management is that it must be a value-added component of helping the organization achieve its mission and goals. Frequently, risk management is seen as almost an exercise in and of itself. This is particularly true if the risk function is considered to be a specialty silo.

Risk management is not the function of a specialist area of an organization. Risk management is everyone's responsibility, and as such, everyone from the board, the management team, through to the front-line workers, whether they be paid or volunteer, should be familiar with the risk principles and the main risk strategies and ideals of the organization. In fact, even key external stakeholders should be made aware of the relevant risk policies that apply to them in their relationship with the organization.

Risk management begins with the strategic mission of a firm and exists solely to help the organization achieve its strategic mission. Risk management is not a "nice to have" function for vague reasons such as that it is trendy or to demonstrate to stakeholders that the organization is trying to manage itself in a responsible and professional way. Risk management is frivolous and a useless but expensive appendage if that is all that it is used for.

A risk management checkup should be done on a periodic basis to ensure that risk management is both adding value and supporting the achievement of the mission and objectives of the organization. If risk management is not adding value, or it is not aiding in the achievement of the objectives, then the risk management policies should be changed or scrapped altogether.

Great risk management is indistinguishable from great management. Ultimately, doesn't every organization, whether for-profit or nonprofit, want to have great management?

An Art or A Science?

Many risk management workshops are conducted as if it were a science lab. Admittedly, some of the concepts and techniques that we will discuss make it seem as if they come direct from a mad scientist's laboratory. The reality is that risk management is as much, if not more than, of an art as it is a science.

The fact that risk management is ultimately about people, and for people, combined with the fact that nonprofits are organizations of a collection of people providing a service to people, makes complexity a key element in risk management. This ever-present aspect of complexity is ultimately what prevents risk management from being a purely objective science.

That risk management is as much of an art as it is a science is particularly true of nonprofits. Nonprofits, as a group, do not have a significant history of risk management. As such there is not a large collective experience from which scientific generalizations can be gleaned. Second, nonprofits tend to be unique in their missions and goals. This, in turn, makes their risks and experiences unique, which again prevents easy scientific generalizations. For-profit corporations are all in a competitive battle against each other, which, although it produces unique strategies and cultures, it also produces a set of common shared experiences from which common trends and best practice strategies can be developed. The lack of scope and scale of most nonprofits is another impediment to making easy generalizations. General management of a nonprofit is more an art than a science. Likewise, risk management is also more an art than a science.

A common mistake in developing risk management is to be too exacting in the process and to set too high of a set of expectations for outcomes. Risk management in the best of circumstances is often an exercise in vagueness, uncertainty, and doubt. In fact, an entire discipline called VUCA (volatility, uncertainty, complexity, and ambiguity) management has developed.

Einstein is reputed to have stated that "elegance is for tailors." The purpose of risk management is to be functional in helping an organization achieve its missions and goals. In the final analysis, it is wise to remember the adage that "it is better to be approximately right than precisely wrong." Risk management is as much of an art as it is a science.

Concluding Thoughts

There are a lot of commonly held beliefs that risk management is more of a science than it is an art. It is believed that risk management is a complicated task that is centered on advanced mathematics and scientific processes. It is widely believed that if a state-of-the-art risk management process is in place, an organization will be risk free. These are all dangerous myths.

The truth is that risk management is ultimately about people in all of their wonderful diversity and complexity. As such, risk management is just as much an art as it is a science. It is about the known knowns as well as the unknown unknowns. That is what makes it such a creative field, but also one that provides a significant operating advantage to the nonprofit that gets it approximately right.

CHAPTER 3

Risk Management Frameworks

Introduction

Imagine a person who tries to eat spaghetti with her bare hands and also assume that she has not seen a fork in her life. The only way she knows to eat spaghetti is to use her fingers. She may still get the same taste as anybody else, but obviously the eating process will be messy and inefficient. A simple tool such as a fork that is probably developed by the scientists of ancient era may make a huge impact. The messy and inefficient process of eating spaghetti may transform into a high performing and delicious activity.

Many—if not most of the—nonprofit organizations face similar problems every day. We can think about daily operations and other management practices as the spaghetti nonprofit organizations need to eat. If nonprofits are not using the management tools that are developed by scientists and practitioners, their situation will not be different than our lady who was not using the fork.

One of the main objectives of this book is to familiarize nonprofit organizations with the scientific tools that are specifically developed for risk management in nonprofit organizations.

One of the most effective management tools is a risk management framework. A framework is a basic conceptual structure which can be used as the main guide or the constitution in a particular management area. This chapter develops a set of four risk management components that form the gradual framework or "Risk Management Tower" for organizing and managing the risks that are unique to nonprofit organizations.

By this stage, most people realize that risk management is a far larger and a far more important task in the operation of a nonprofit organization than they likely ever considered it to be. To help organize all of the moving parts of a comprehensive risk management plan, most organizations will adopt a risk framework. A risk framework gives a structure and a level of overall guidance to the risk management process. A risk framework helps to illustrate how the various parts of a risk management strategy are connected and how each piece is central to the success and effectiveness of the plan. However, it must be remembered that a risk framework is just a general guide, and each organization should adapt to their own specific needs and objectives.

There are two widely covered enterprise risk management frameworks that are widely accepted by many for-profit organizations. We present these frameworks in the first section of this chapter and then present a framework, called the ViStA framework, that we believe is well suited for most nonprofit groups.

Two Global Frameworks: The COSO and ISO Frameworks

In response to the corporate for-profit debacles such as Worldcom and Enron that characterized the early part of the 1990s, there was a generic call for better management and by extension better risk management. Two somewhat similar frameworks came to be widely accepted, and the field of enterprise risk management, or ERM, was created. In part, these frameworks grew out of legislation, most particularly the Sarbanes–Oxley Act in the United States.

The Sarbanes–Oxley Act, more commonly known as SOX, laid out some principles for corporate governance and control that United States-based corporations needed to follow in order to be publicly traded. What developed from this was a realization that risk management was not a luxury but a necessary component of running a prudently managed organization.

The two frameworks were the International Standards Organization 31000 standard, commonly called ISO 31000, and the Committee of Sponsoring Organizations of the Treadway Commission, which is more commonly known as COSO. The ISO 31000 framework was initially developed in 2009, and updated in 2018, while the COSO framework debuted in 2004 and was updated in 2017.

The original COSO framework was a cube. On the front face on the cube were eight steps to risk management. These eight steps were (1) Internal Environment, (2) Objective Setting, (3) Event Identification, (4) Risk Assessment, (5) Risk Response, (6) Control Activities, (7) Information and Communication, and (8) Monitoring. These eight steps were the core of the risk management framework, and were to be applied to the (1) Strategic, (2) Operations, (3) Reporting, and (4) Compliance activities of the firm. These four components composed the top face of the cube. The side face of the cube consisted of four components: (1) Entity-level, (2) Division, (3) Business Unit, and (4) Subsidiary level.

The original COSO cube was intended to provide a holistic scheme for examining and managing the risks of the firm not only throughout the firm but also at each individual level. It was an accounting and reporting-based framework, which was heavily influenced by a similar framework for reporting that was also instituted by the same group.

The original COSO cube thus consisted of 128 individual cells (eight front face slices, four top face slices, and four side face slices) for the firm to manage. It was quite a bureaucratic task if one were to implement the framework in all of its full detail. Furthermore, it was not at all clear how the framework could be used to answer the question whether the risk management of an organization was improving. It was common for the risk objectives of an organization to get lost in the mass of details of the framework. While the framework was great for consultants who were billed by the hour, it created a risk function that was more bureaucratic than a functioning part of business operations.

The original ISO 31000 framework was somewhat similar to the front face of the COSO cube. It consisted of a five-step process of (1) establishing the context of an organization, (2) risk assessment (which consisted of risk identification, risk analysis, and risk evaluation), (3) risk treatment, and these three elements connected by (4) communication and consultation as well as (5) monitoring and review.

The two frameworks obviously had a lot of commonalities, but they differed in how comprehensive and specific they were. The somewhat more streamlined ISO 31000 framework caught on more outside of the United States, while the COSO framework was more widely adopted within the United States, as it fitted more with the Sarbanes–Oxley regulation.

The COSO framework was redone in 2017, and ISO 31000 in 2018. Both revisions focus on less rigidity in their frameworks and more fluidity in how risk management should be conducted. While including less details, the revised frameworks focus more on how risk management should focus on value and performance for an organization. There is also an enhanced realization that risk management is an interactive as well as iterative process that is context specific that does not lend itself to a one-size-fits-all framework. These are themes that we heartily endorse for nonprofits and try to live up to in our suggested framework that follows.

The ViStA Risk Framework

ViStA Core

The ViStA risk framework is a four-level risk management framework that we have specifically developed for nonprofits. Level one of the ViStA framework, the ViStA core, is shown in Figure 3.1. The framework

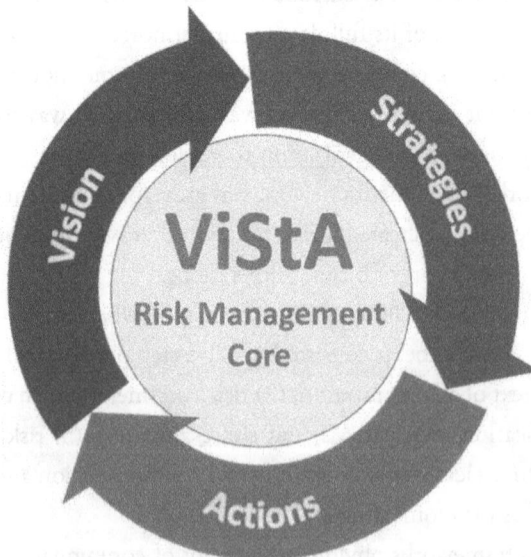

Figure 3.1 ViStA core

illustrates that risk management is at the center of the vision, strategies, and actions of an organization. The risk management plan is to be both informed by and supportive of the vision, strategies, and actions. As a simple principle, all strategies and activities of a nonprofit organization have to support the vision of the nonprofit. This will not only ensure that all strategies are aligned in the same direction but also ensure that limited resources will be used properly and effectively.

Risk Parameters Trio

The second level of the ViStA framework is shown in Figure 3.2. It adds the risk parameters trio to the ViStA core. Here the characteristics of the risks are included; specifically, the impact of the risk, the probability or likelihood of the occurrence of risk, and the amount of control it is believed that the organization has over risk.

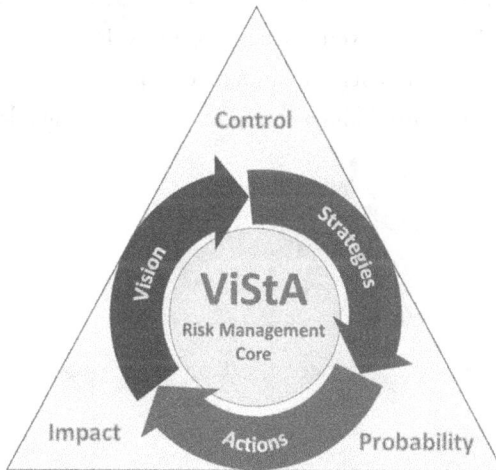

Figure 3.2 Risk parameters trio

Probability is the measure that shows how likely a particular risk will occur and is generally expressed as a percentage or a number between 0 and 1. Expressing probability as low–medium–high ordinal scale, or on a quantitative scale between 1 and 5, where 1 is the lowest and 5 is the highest likelihood, is also popular especially for risk management.

In our framework the probability of risk is measured between 0 and 100, which is basically the average of grades given by board members, the executive director, and other managers who are familiar with the organization and the risk it faces. Some concepts for the process of actual measurement will be presented in Chapter 5.

The second parameter of the risk parameters trio is called "impact" and is related with the consequences of risk. Similar to risk itself, impact may also be good or bad as discussed in Chapter 1. Due to this reason, impact needs to be measured on a scale with both positive and negative measures where positive means beneficial impact and negative represents harmful impact.

The last parameter of the risk parameters trio is "control," which indicates the level of influence or control that the organization believes it has in managing a particular risk. Control, like impact, is a relative measure and can be measured on a numerical scale or an ordinal scale such as low, medium, and high.

To implement the risk parameters trio, organizations often create a "risk map." Figure 3.3 illustrates a risk map, where the horizontal axis represents the impact, the vertical axis represents the probability, and the size of the circle represents the amount of control, with a large circle representing little control and a small circle representing a large amount of control.[1]

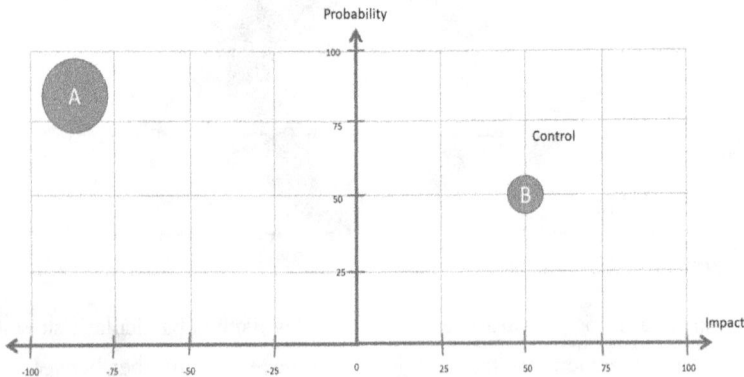

Figure 3.3 Risk parameters trio risk map

---

[1]More details on risk maps and their construction will be covered in Chapter 5, "Risk Analytics."

From Figure 3, we observe that risk A has a large amount of negative impact risk, and a large probability of occurring. Furthermore, the organization believes it has a small amount of control over the risk. Risk B, conversely, has medium positive impact, a medium probability of occurring, and the organization has a medium amount of control.

Stakeholder Trio

The third level continues to build on the structure by adding the stakeholder trio. The stakeholder trio takes the considerations of the stakeholders of the organization into account. Specifically, the stakeholder trio includes the risk interests and risk effects of the service providers, the sponsors, and the beneficiaries of the organization. The stakeholder trio of the framework is illustrated in Figure 3.4.

Figure 3.4 Stakeholder trio

In most of the cases the risk stakeholders are not different than (just) stakeholders. However, using a risk-specific terminology has two main benefits. First, it works like a filter that forces everyone to think from the viewpoint of risk. In other words, it helps nonprofit organizations to focus on risk. Second, the list of risk stakeholders may be different (or rather be a subgroup of) all stakeholders in specific cases.

One key objective about the risk stakeholders is to convince them to become risk partners. The output may be addressed as risk partnership and indicates a situation where risk is shared and managed jointly. This should, of course, go without saying for the staff and volunteers of the organization, but if other stakeholders buy in as well, then it is likely that everyone benefits.

Risk partnership is an effective strategic tool for nonprofit organizations and enhances the involvement of related stakeholders in managing risk. For example, a charity that experiences difficulties at finding more volunteers may cooperate with its current volunteers and get their support to find others. This process of current volunteers influencing future volunteers happens automatically at certain level in many charities. However, to be able to call it an effective risk partnership it has to be managed in a systematic way.[2]

Risk Management Tower

The ViStA framework is completed with level four, risk management tower. Risk management tower takes the previous three levels of the framework and places them in the main risk management tasks of risk identification, risk analysis and mapping, risk treatment and risk governance (Figure 3.5).

The ViStA risk framework is a vista or a forward-looking model that systematically covers the main tasks required of the risk operations of nonprofits. It is designed to be simple, actionable, applicable, and relatable to nonprofit organizations. It covers the necessary elements of a comprehensive framework and nothing more. It is as streamlined as possible. In the following sections we elaborate on each of the levels of the ViStA model.

---

[2]More details on stakeholder management and risk partnerships will be covered in Chapter 10, "Partnerships and Stakeholder Engagement."

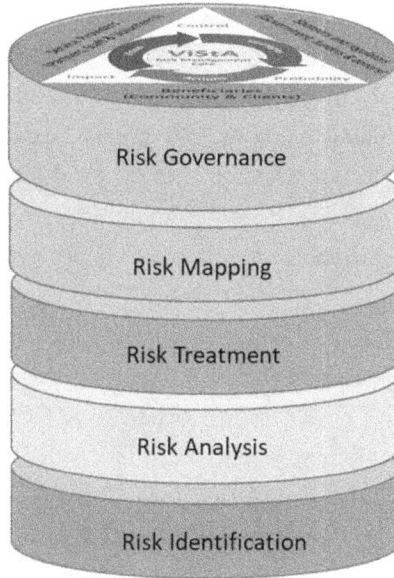

Figure 3.5 Risk management tower

ViStA Core

The ViStA core is composed of three elements: the organization's vision, the organization's strategies, and the organization's actions. Risk management is at the center of these three fundamental operations—which should be the fundamental operations of any organization whether a for-profit organization or a nonprofit organization.

With this specific design, it is explicit that risk management is not an add-on activity but one that is at the very core of the organization's activities. As stated previously, risk management has a direct relationship with the vision, strategies, and actions of the organization. Just as risk management helps to inform and guide the development of the vision, strategies, and actions, so the vision, strategies, and actions set the mandate, priorities, and activities of risk management.

It is important to have a well-defined statement of each of the elements of the ViStA core. This includes risk management objectives. The organization should be clear about what the objectives of the risk management implementation are to be. As will be discussed in the section on risk management tower, the determination and setting of risk management objectives is a critical function of the board and senior management with input from all relevant stakeholders. Just as fuzzy thinking on the objectives of risk management is detrimental to the effectiveness of the organization, so fuzzy thinking on the vision, strategies, and actions is.

There are many reasonable objectives for the risk management function. They range from the basic of simply achieving regulatory compliance through to assisting the organization becoming world-class in effectiveness.

Despite our passion for risk management, and despite the fact that we believe that risk management is a key component in helping nonprofits achieve their objectives, we believe that the ambitiousness of risk management objectives should be in line with the scope and scale of the operations of the organization itself. Too often we have observed that well-meaning board members, in their zeal to make their nonprofit world-class, have pushed for large, risk management systems designed for much larger for-profit organizations to be implemented in the much smaller nonprofit whose board they sit on. The risk management operations that they are pushing for would simply dwarf all of the other activities of the organization. The main goal of risk management is to help and serve the organization in achieving its objectives and mission, not to be a major operational and resource drag in doing so.

The Risk Management Trio

The risk management trio develops the concept that each element of risk has an impact element, a probability element, and a control element. For each element of the core, the vision, strategies, and actions, the risks of the organization have a range of impact, a probability of occurring, and a level of control that the organization has over that risk.

Determining the level of impact, probability, and control can be a very subjective exercise in risk analysis. This is particularly so for a nonprofit where so many of the important risks are qualitative in nature. The major concept to remember here is that it is the identification of the risks that is critical. There is a tendency to only identify those risks that can be easily measured or quantified. While it is important to have some idea of the impacts, probability, and control level of risks, the reality is that for most risks an accurate measure of these characteristics is not possible or realistic to obtain. The important element is to be aware of and to identify the important risks regardless of whether they can be accurately measured or not.

Too many organizations get so caught up in these measurements that they miss the forest for the trees. For instance, one nonprofit that we were asked to help had a board member who insisted that all risks be measured to a 99 percent level of accuracy. The organization was a health care facility for disadvantaged people. The workers and volunteers at the facility had developed a comprehensive listing of their risks and had a reasonable handle on how to classify them as whether they were low, medium, or high impact and similar estimates for the probabilities. The unrealistic demand for precision put a great deal of unnecessary stress on the staff who were trying their best to implement a practical and useful risk management system. The board member had a background in banking—where measurement of financial risks can conceivably be measured with a high degree of precision. (Whether the precision is accurate or justified is a totally other matter as evidenced by the number of financial institutions that get into difficulty with their risk management practices and understanding.)

A key element to remember when measuring risks and their impact is the adage usually credited to John Maynard Keynes who stated that "it is better to be approximately right than precisely wrong." Obviously, one should aim to measure precisely when it is easy and appropriate to do, but otherwise a high, medium, or low classification is usually more than good enough. In a similar theme, it is important to remember that just because you can measure a risk accurately does not mean that you understand that particular risk, and the converse is true as well; just because you cannot measure it accurately does not necessarily mean that you do not understand it.

The Stakeholder Trio

The stakeholder trio acknowledges that the organization exists for its stakeholders, namely, its service providers, its beneficiaries, and the sponsors of the organization. A principle that will emphasized throughout this book is that at the heart of risk management is people. Organizations are created by people and for people. This is particularly true in the case of nonprofits. It is also true that risk management is for the people—the stakeholders of the organization.

People are the main cause of risks, and people are the means for dealing with risk, and people are the ones who bear both the positive and the negative consequences of risk. Just as there is no more important part in the management of an organization than the stakeholders, so there is no more important part of risk management than the people component.

One of the difficult parts of risk management is that different people will perceive risk differently. Rarely are important risks completely subjective. Even rarer are the situations where people have aligned risk appetites. This makes getting agreement on risk very difficult.

The stakeholders of a nonprofit will have different needs and desires, and these needs and desires will involve different risks and different levels of risk. Thus it is vital to realize that the ViStA core that defines the risk management objectives and the vision, strategies, and actions of the organization are so important. Fuzzy work on the ViStA core will produce difficulties in latter stages of development of the risk management plan and particularly so when it comes to dealing with the risk management of the stakeholders. (It should go without saying that a vague statement of the ViStA core will also have significant implications for the successful achievement of the mission of the nonprofit.)

Risk Management Tower

Risk management tower is the final component that both surrounds and provides a base on which the rest of the ViStA components exist. Risk management tower has as its base the risk governance of the organization.

Much more will be said about risk governance in Chapter 11, but for now it suffices to say that risk governance is the objective setting and the accountability center for the risk management operations of a firm. Setting risk management objectives is the obvious starting point for all of the risk management activities. Risk management objectives should be set by the board and senior management after consultation with a representative set of the stakeholders. Like all of the components of the risk management system, risk objectives should be reviewed on a periodic basis to ensure that they are still relevant and helping the organization as expected.

Two more major functions that need to be mentioned at this point regarding risk governance are assigning accountability and efficient communication of risk awareness throughout the organization. Governance implies accountability, but risk management accountability cannot rest solely with the board or senior management, or even with a dedicated risk management unit. Risk management must be a shared responsibility for it to be effective. Yes, there will be certain tasks that are the responsibility of certain members or units of the organization, but broader risks need to be shared. It is part of good risk governance to have the risk accountability clearly communicated and understood by all relevant stakeholders.

Related to accountability is the communication aspect of risk governance. There needs to be a system for risk objectives, risk monitoring, risk policies, and effectiveness of the risk management program to be communicated throughout the organization.

The top layer of risk management tower is risk identification. Risk analysis is a key step in risk management. Our first law of risk management states that the mere fact that you acknowledge that a risk exists automatically improves the management of it, regardless of whether it is a positive risk or a negative risk. Risk identification is covered in the following chapter.

The second layer of risk management tower is risk analysis and mapping. Risk analysis and mapping is determining the impact, probabilities, and control mechanisms of the risks identified and having a mechanism for understanding and prioritizing such risks. Essentially it is where the risk triangle gets measured and prioritized. Risk analysis and mapping is covered in Chapter 5.

Risk treatment is the stage of deciding how to manage each risk. It is where the decisions are made as to what tactics, if any, will be adopted to mitigate the risk if it is a negative risk or how to capitalize and leverage the risk if it is a positive risk. Risk treatment is covered in more detail in Chapter 9.

Concluding Thoughts

Risk management frameworks are a valuable aid to initiating and developing a risk management program. However, there are some pitfalls to relying too heavily on any given risk framework.

The first pitfall to avoid is to prevent risk management becoming a slave to a risk framework. Many organizations choose and implement a framework with the best of intentions. Soon, however, risk management exists to satisfy the framework rather than to satisfy the risk management needs of the organization, and more specifically risk management is no longer functioning for effectively achieving the mission and goals of the organization. This is a trap that an organization is particularly prone to fall into when the framework is chosen for regulatory or compliance reasons rather than for managerial reasons. Admittedly, a framework can help ensure compliance, but compliance is not necessarily risk management.

A second trap to avoid is picking a framework that is too elaborate or functionally inappropriate for the scale and scope of the organization. The risk management framework that is appropriate for a local Little League baseball organization with an all-volunteer staff will be very different for an international nonprofit that deals in the health care sector with a multimillion-dollar budget in several countries and a complement of paid professional staff and management.

Once a framework is in place, it is important to remember that having a risk framework in place does not mean that an organization is actually practicing risk management. Frequently, organizations implicitly believe that if they have a risk framework implemented, they can forget about thinking about and practicing risk management; they fantastically and often tragically believe that the framework will magically do the day-to-day tough work of actually managing risk. It is the equivalent of someone paying for a gym membership and then believing that they no longer have to watch their diet and can forever thereafter forgo exercising. Risk management is an active and ongoing activity. A risk framework, by contrast, is static and inert.

Related to this is risk homeostasis. Basically, the principle of risk homeostasis is a phenomenon that people will act so as to keep the overall risk level constant. Thus, if people believe that there is a strong risk framework in place, they are likely to take imprudent risks that they would not otherwise take. Just be aware that a risk framework does not eliminate the need to be risk-intelligent in your actions.

CHAPTER 4

Risks of Nonprofit Organizations

Risk in a for-profit organization, with some important exceptions, mostly come down to the effect on the variability of profits or cash flows of the firm. These risks are, for the most part, relatively easy to quantify. By contrast, in a nonprofit organization, the key risks are those that deal with the variability of the obtainment of objectives, or the mission of the nonprofit. This risk is generally much more difficult to quantify and is generally quite subjective and open to interpretation. This creates a fundamental difference in how risk is managed in a for-profit, versus a nonprofit organization.

A second difference is that the risks of a for-profit firm are likely shared among members of the industry, but given the local size and scope of many nonprofits, this industry sharing of knowledge is somewhat limited. In a similar vein, for-profits will generally have a specialized function to deal with risk identification, measurement, and communication; for instance, most major for-profit organizations have a specialized risk department. However, due to lack of resources or awareness, the specialized function of a risk department is likely to be nonexistent in most nonprofits.

A third key distinction between the risks of the for-profit corporation and a nonprofit is that many of the financial risks of the for-profit firm can be hedged directly through financial hedges or risk sharing vehicles such as market syndication. Such methods are not available for the major risks that nonprofits need to manage.

A final distinction in risk management is that for-profit firms have the means and incentive to mitigate and manage their risks through diversification of products or services offered, diversification of geographies in which they operate, or even diversification of managerial and operating strategies. The single-minded purpose of nonprofits limits the amount of diversification that they can use for risk management.

Many of the modern risks of corporations though are also similar to those of the nonprofit. This is particularly true for reputational risk as social media becomes such a major part of the core base of this critical risk. Corporations and nonprofits also have similar operational risk in terms of managing people and their operations. However even in managing people there are differences in the incentives for behavior that a for-profit can use that are generally not available to the nonprofit.

The one characteristic that is common to both for-profit and nonprofit organizations is that prudent management of risks can pay big returns in terms of the resulting effectiveness of the organization. This chapter introduces the breadth of risks faced by a nonprofit in order to provide an appreciation of the scope and variety. Later chapters will discuss the various classes of risk more fully.

Risk Identification and the First Law of Risk Management

The first step in risk management is to identify the risks. This is often much easier said than done. In our daily lives, we routinely identify, measure, and manage a wide variety of risks unconsciously. In fact, it is generally only when a risk drastically changes that we bother to consciously notice it at all. For instance, consider your commute home from work today. How many people that you saw on your commute could you describe for us? Unless you are an unusually sociable person, it is likely the only people you can describe are those who were dressed outrageously or had some other distinguishing characteristics such as a peacock in full plume sitting on their head. The same is true of risk; we generally only notice it when it is unusual or unexpected, and by then it is often too late to do anything about it.

Risk identification is key to developing an effective risk management program. Our first law of risk management states that the mere fact that you acknowledge that a risk exists automatically improves your management of it. This can be expanded to: The mere fact that you acknowledge that a risk exists, automatically increases the probability and magnitude of it occurring if it is a good risk, and likewise automatically decreases the probability and severity of it occurring if it is a negative risk. That is a bold and very powerful law, but one that we have rarely seen violated.

Risk identification is the start of the process that includes prioritizing risks and then deciding what action, if any, go take to manage the risk. Risk identification should be kept separate from risk prioritization, as prioritization can only be completed when the full range of risks have been identified. If prioritization or judgment about risks is made at the identification stage, then there is a high probability that some risks will be summarily dismissed as being insignificant, while they are in reality very significant, and other risks will be given excess priority due to familiarity or some other cognitive bias. Additionally, a rush to prioritize risks will not allow one to consider the patterns and the relationships between the risks.

Given that one should be careful to not prejudge risks, it is useful when identifying risk to remember that there are three fundamental questions that will be dealt with in the risk management process; what can happen, when can it happen, and how much of an effect can it have.

To properly identify risks throughout the organization requires three elements. They are creativity, a diverse set of perspectives and a systematic scan of the horizon. Creativity is central to risk identification. In conducting risk workshops, we reiterate a phrase that has been attributed in various forms to a variety of great thinkers: "an idea that at first blush which does not appear to be ridiculous is probably not worth considering." Another great way to get creative is to build stories that assume that the organization has not met their goals and then create the backstory that describes the reasons why the goals were not met. Just remember though that risk has an upside and a downside, so you need stories to explain how the organization outperformed as well as underperformed their goals. You need to identify the potentially good risks just as much as you need to identify the bad risks.

Related to creativity is having a diversity of views in risk identification. Cognitive diversity, identity diversity, and functional diversity in the background of the team doing the risk identification stage are all important forms of diversity. The risk identification team should not only be composed of people who think differently, and have cultural, racial, and gender diversity, but also different functional diversity in that they perform diverse tasks both in their professional careers as well in the tasks that they perform for the nonprofit.

Diversity is important in risk identification for many reasons. The most obvious is to avoid groupthink and thus a blind eye to significant risks. Lack of diversity also leads to bias in not only identifying, but also in assessing risks. Functional and cognitive diversity allows the risk identification process to both see and understand risks that would likely not be observed or appreciated by a less diverse group.

It is important to realize that not every risk will be identified. New risks arise, and accidents (yes—both happy and sad accidents) do happen. The universe of risks is infinite and in constant flux. It is not reasonable, nor realistic to expect that the full range of risks will be uncovered. However, by performing a series of periodic risk identification scans, the organization will be much better prepared to manage risk and take advantage of our first law of risk management for those risks that do arise—even those that the risk identification process missed or passed over.

One of the best ways to ensure a complete and thorough compilation of the risks is to develop a taxonomy or classification of risks. There are a variety of ways that this can be done, which is the focus of the rest of this chapter.

Strategic Risk

Strategic risk is the uncertainty that the strategy chosen will lead to unexpected outcomes and thus the organization being unable to achieve their objectives. As with all other risks, it must be remembered that strategic risk could be positive or negative. The organization could choose a strategy that luckily for them produces outcomes far better than expected.

For a nonprofit, strategic risk is generally taken lightly. For most nonprofits, the mission of the organization is assumed to be well known. The reality is that many nonprofits do not have a written mission statement, or if they do, it is interpreted in different ways by different stakeholders.

We have been on several different nonprofit boards and observed that different stakeholders have a very different interpretation of the mission—and that is among the stakeholders who are board members and thus had a hand in crafting the mission. This is perhaps the biggest, and most fundamental risk in a nonprofit. If there is not common understanding and interpretation of the mission—again, which is assumed to be well known—then there cannot be agreement with the strategic initiatives that the organization should take.

However, that does not imply that the top-level strategy to achieve the mission is a given, or even what the objectives of that mission should be. Different stakeholders and participants in the nonprofit may have very different concepts on the objectives of the mission and how to achieve those objectives. Often this means that strategic risk begins with managing the mission and the objective setting processes of the organization.

For instance, consider the nonprofit that manages Little League Baseball for a county. The mission might be as simple and as innocent as to promote Little League Baseball in the county. To some stakeholders however this means that the objective is to produce Little League Baseball teams that successfully compete in state and national tournaments. To another group of stakeholders, it means that as many different kids as possible are engaged in playing organized baseball. A third group may be more concerned that kids are playing baseball regardless whether it is organized baseball or pickup games in the schoolyard without umpires and official record-keepers. All of these admirable objectives require a very different operating strategy that will produce conflict among themselves.

Although strategic risk should, at least conceptually, be much simpler for a nonprofit that generally has a sole purpose for existing, the reality in our experience is that nonprofit organizations often have passionate stakeholders with widely different opinions on what the strategy of the organization should be. Thus strategic risk begins with widely different views on what the objectives should be. Without a clear set of objectives, there is almost certain to be strategic risk—and it almost certainly will not be upside strategic risk!

A related component to strategic risk for a nonprofit that we have frequently observed is that everyone agrees with the mission statement, but the various constituent stakeholders all interpret it to their viewpoint.

This results in everyone believing that the objectives are well understood and agreed on by all, when anything but is the truer reality. This set of false assumptions leads to perhaps the biggest strategic risk of all. We have observed that several nonprofit boards get into either heated debates or collapse into total confusion when asked what exactly the objectives of the organization are.

Assuming that the objectives are known and agreed upon, there is still the strategic risk issue of how best to achieve those objectives. Strategy setting is anything but an exact science and many nonprofit organizers have limited experience in setting and implementing a strategy. Strategic risk is not just a function of choosing a strategy, which itself is a daunting task fraught with risk. Strategic risk also encompasses the implementation risk of the strategy. It is risky to figure out what one should do (the strategy setting), and it is risky to actually be able to implement the strategy as intended.

Doing a risk analysis of the strategic risks is a very important and useful part of the risk management process. As will be stressed later, the risk management process has at its primary function to aid in the achievement of the strategy and the objectives. Thus, risk management and strategy are completely interrelated. Risk management exists solely to bolster the strategy. Second, risk management thinking can aid in the development of alternative strategies and in the ultimate choice of strategy. This is a process that adds important rigor to the strategy setting process and greatly improves the likelihood of successful outcomes. Thirdly, strategy should be chosen with the risk management implications in mind. The relationship between strategy and risk management is a two-way street. Each informs and reinforces the other.

Too often we have observed organizations, both for-profit and especially nonprofit organizations ignore risk management when strategy setting. Sadly, we also frequently observe both types of organizations completely skip the strategy and objective setting process but simply assuming a given strategy and set of objectives. This leads to mass confusion, inefficiency, loss of morale, and a general mess that always ends badly, unless and until rectified.

Explicitly acknowledging strategic risk, and the fact that the strategy (and tactics) chosen may not align with the mission statement, forces an organization to create a clear and unambiguous understanding of its mission. While there may be differences of opinion about the appropriateness of specific strategies, explicitly including strategic risk helps to clarify the mission, and helps to illuminate that all strategies to accomplish the mission have risks.

Operational Risk

Operational risk is generally described as those risks that arise from the people and the processes of the organization. As such, operational risk encompasses a wide variety and types of risk. Operational risks tend to be idiosyncratic to the organization. They tend to be a unique combination of the strategies, the culture, the people and the history of activities of the organization.

Operational risk is one area of risk identification in particular that needs to have diversity in the committee that is involved in the risk identification exercise. The people actually doing the functions are the ones who are generally best positioned to know and understand the operational risks. Conversely, the people overseeing the operations can often observe aspects of operations that those "in the trenches" miss due to their closeness to the activities in question. Finally, the beneficiaries of the organization will observe and be aware of a whole different set of risks and will have their own interpretation of the potential impact of the risks.

Operational risks are covered in detail in Chapter 7.

Financial Risk

Financial risk is the variability or uncertainty in the finances of the nonprofit. For many nonprofits financial risk is a major and ongoing concern. Essentially, financial risk is concerned with the question of whether or not the financial resources will be available when needed to carry out the strategic plan. Given that the vast majority of nonprofits are financially constrained, this is generally a negative risk. However, we have observed that when nonprofits receive a windfall, such as an unexpectedly generous donation, that the uncertainty and disputes about how to spend the windfall can be catastrophic.

Financial risk identification begins with the budgeting process. Financial risk often determines the strategic risk and vice-versa. The more ambitious the strategic plan, the more stress tends to be placed on the financial heath and budgeting of the organization.

The second aspect of financial risk is the variability of the revenue sources. The variability of donations, grants, revenue generating activities comprise this aspect of financial risk. Netting the risk of the expenditures, with the risk of the revenues gives the total financial risk exposure.

Generally speaking, the greater the strategic risk, the lower the financial risk of the organization should be. Conversely, the lower the financial risk, the greater the strategic risk that the organization may consider taking on as its target level of risk. Financial risk is covered more fully in Chapter 6.

Reputational Risk

Reputational risk is the uncertainty of how the nonprofit will be perceived among its stakeholders. Reputational risk is critical for most nonprofits, especially if they principally rely upon donations for their continued existence. Reputational risk is key in the willingness of donors to give, and stakeholders to engage in the achievement of the organization's goals.

A classic example of a changing reputational risk is the Lance Armstrong Foundation. The yellow "Livestrong" wrist band was a huge fundraising and reputational success for the foundation and its mission "to improve the lives of cancer survivors and those affected by cancer."[1] The yellow bracelets became a social phenomenon that was widely recognized and praised. The acceptance and adoption of the bracelets were beyond even the wildest and most optimistic of expectations. The famous cyclist, a cancer survivor himself, was a powerful and popular spokesperson for the foundation that bore his name. However, after it was revealed that Lance Armstrong had cheated by blood doping while a professional cyclist, his position as spokesperson became a serious issue. Just as quickly, the ubiquitous yellow bracelets became a symbol for fraud and dropped out of favor with the public even more rapidly that their surprising meteoric rise

---

[1]https://en.wikipedia.org/wiki/Livestrong_Foundation (assessed May 16, 2019).

had been. The foundation eventually dropped the Lance Armstrong name and became known as the Livestrong Foundation. While this is a drastic, and high profile example, it clearly illustrates the importance and the fickleness of reputational risk.

Reputation is both a complicated and a complex issue. It can be affected by many factors. The factors do not even have to be real or true. Perceptions can be based on rumors or speculation with little or no basis in reality or fact. Reputation can also spiral out of control, particularly in the age of social media. Social media is used very effectively to promote and enhance the reputation of many organizations. Misused, either intentionally or unintentionally, social media can also quickly and permanently tarnish the reputation of any type of organization. Having sound and robust social media policies in place is a key component of a risk management plan. It is also prudent to have a crisis social media management plan given the importance and prevalence of social media tools in today's society.

Human Capital Risk

Human capital risk is the risk of having the right people performing the right tasks. Human capital risk extends to the recruitment, training, and retention of staff and volunteers as well as management and board members. Previously we discussed that operational risk includes people and processes. Since the staffing on nonprofits is so critical, we have specifically broken out the human capital piece of operational risk as a separate risk on its own. We will still discuss the people risk in operations, but for human capital risk we focus on are the right people in the right places, doing the right tasks that they are assigned.

Staffing of nonprofits is a delicate balance. Generally, the staffing is a mix of paid employees and volunteers. Furthermore, both the paid and unpaid staff are likely to be highly committed to the cause of the organization. This creates scenarios of potential imbalance of incentives. In a for-profit organization, staff can be motivated to take certain actions through their compensation incentive, or the risk of losing their position. However, most of the staff at nonprofits are either unpaid, or underpaid, so the usual organizing incentive of pay is not present. The combination of passion for the mission, and lack of financial incentives, gives rise to the risk that necessary, but boring and unrelated tasks that are not directly tied to the mission, such as risk management activities, may not be attended to in the same way as they would in a for-profit organization.

Human capital risk is covered at length in Chapter 7.

Legal Risk

Legal risk is the risk that regulatory, compliance and legal necessities will not be appropriately dealt with. Legal risk in particular can be catastrophic for a nonprofit. A major lawsuit, even an unsuccessful one, can severely hamper, or even put a nonprofit out of existence.

Most people understand the importance and potential impact of legal risk as well as reputational risk. The difference is in the nuances of them. Reputational risk can be more subtle, and often is less objective than legal risk. (Admittedly, legal risk can also be very subtle as well.)

Legal and reputational risk has taken on a new nature with the rise of social media. Social media is a primary way that organizations get their message out to their stakeholders and to the public at large. Social media is thus a huge asset for the typical nonprofit. However, social media is also where an organization is exposed to cybercrime and social media trolls that can ruin an organization's financial or reputational situation in a flash and even open them up to significantly negative legal implications. Managing social media risk and cyberrisk has thus become a major risk management project for many organizations; a task that many are ill-prepared to manage.

Legal and reputational risks are discussed in Chapter 8.

External versus Internal Risks

One useful way of classifying risks is based on those that are internal to the organization and those that are external. Obviously, these are two classes of risk, but the focus is so often on the internal risks; those that the organization believes that they can control, or at least conceptually control. The issue with this thinking is that few organizations exist as an island unto themselves. Organizations exist for their service to the larger society and thus external risks are every bit as important as internal risks.

As already alluded to, external risks differ from internal risks in the level of control the organization has. While an organization may not be able to control the external environment that it operates in, it can build the systems and practices it needs to be resilient to any external risks. Simply because one cannot control a risk, does not mean that one should not do what one can to prepare oneself to manage that risk if it should arise.

Complex versus Complicated

In Chapter 1, the difference between issues that are complicated and those that are complex were discussed. This is a critical distinction for risk management as many risks faced by nonprofit organizations are of a complex nature, and thus must be handled quite differently.

As previously discussed, complexity arises when you have stakeholders (which could be individuals, or groups of people), who can interact (which could be face-to-face, through social media, or in a wide variety of other ways), and who can adapt or change their opinions, actions or beliefs. When these characteristics are present, the phenomena of emergence arises. Emergence is a leaderless movement that behaves in a way that patterns can be seen, but the patterns are random and unpredictable. The financial markets exhibit emergence, as do consumer fads, such as fidget spinners or popular music trends. Politics exhibit emergence, such as the rise of the Arab Spring in late 2010, or movements such as the hashtag MeToo movement. Complexity and emergence is like the reactions of a mob of people. Outcomes are unpredictable, and leaders are very limited in how much they can affect or control the actions of the mob. (Again—it is important to remember that mobs are not only negative, but can also produce positive outcomes.)

Complexity in risk management arises in virtually all types of risks, but especially those external risks that involve reputational risk. Complexity is also implicit in strategic risk and the cultural risk that exists within the organization. Complexity can play a major role in the spirit of workers and volunteers of an organization and impact on the effectiveness of the organization of carrying out its mission. Of course complexity is also inherent in social media and cyberrisks.

The main thing to realize about complex risks is that they need to be managed differently. Complicated systems work by rules and laws, such as the rules and laws of physics, or the rules and laws of regulation. Complicated issues can thus be managed or solved by applying the best practices that arise from understanding the underlying rules or laws. Managing a complicated issue is like managing a mechanical watch; the watch works based on the laws of the enclosed springs and gears, and if you set and wind the watch appropriately, the watch will perform as expected. Complex risks on the other hand have no underlying rules or laws. Complex risks need to be handled in a holistic fashion; reductionist thinking does not work for them. The best that one can do with complex risks is to attempt to manage them; solving them is not possible due to the random element that is involved.[2]

In a way it would be nice if all risks were complicated in nature. Then one could simply apply best practice (perhaps even buy a computer app), and all risks could automatically be solved or maximally managed. Organizations of all types however, and especially nonprofits, exist to allow people to serve people. As long as people are the focus, there will be elements of complexity. Complexity is a reality in risk management.

There are two positive aspects to complexity. First complexity responds to the first law of risk management, and thus simply by acknowledging complex risks, the management of them automatically is improved. Second, complex risks can also produce unexpectedly good outcomes. That is complexity can be managed positively. The story of the yellow "Live Strong" wristbands that became a phenomenon in the 1990s, and created both a major fundraising and reputational boost for the Lance Armstrong Foundation is an example of a complex phenomenon that is a classic example of emergence helping a nonprofit.

---

[2]More detail and ideas on managing complex situations can be found in R. Nason. 2017. *It's Not Complicated: The Art and Science of Complexity in Business"* (Toronto, Canada: University of Toronto Press).

Concluding Thoughts

In this chapter we have gone through a listing of the various types or categories of risks that an organization faces. The chapters that follow will go into more details about the specifics of the major risks and how to deal with them. The purpose here has been to illustrate the wide variety of risks that exist in order to develop an appreciation that risk management is a holistic task.

Risk management requires skills in many different areas of management. Although the focus of most nonprofits is very narrow, their risks can be broad in scope. This statement has several implications. The first is that risk management is not just a task for a few specialists, but instead ideally involves the cooperation and participation of all stakeholders. Second, that risk requires creativity and a generalist outlook.

It may be intimidating to realize the breadth of the various risks that an organization is exposed to. However, it is best to keep in mind that risk is a two-way street; it is the possibility that bad or good things may happen. Additionally, remember our first law of risk management: the mere fact that you acknowledge that a risk exists automatically improvers your management of it.

CHAPTER 5

Risk Analytics

When we think about risk management and risk analytics, we think of Formula 1 race cars—arguably the most sophisticated form of racing in the world. A Formula 1 team succeeds or fails based on its use of analytics. The proper collection, analysis, and implementing changes based on data can be the difference between winning a race, finishing tenth, or even more tragic outcomes such as precipitating an accident. It is why data companies use Formula 1 cars so often in their advertising.

A Formula 1 team has many different layers of analytics and many different types of data that it analyzes. There is timing data that is measured to the one-thousandth of a second, and then there is the much more imprecise "feel" of the driver who complains that the car does not "feel" balanced. There is data that needs to be acted on immediately, such as data that the driver sees on their dashboard; there is data that the pit crew sees, such as tire temperature, which guides them in telling the driver when to make a pit stop for a tire change; there is forecast data such as simulations, which make predictions on how they will finish if they pit now versus deciding to pit later; and there is a variety of data points that are collected to be analyzed when the race season is over and new aerodynamic designs are contemplated.

Likewise, the use of data for risk management by a nonprofit can also dramatically change their outcomes for the better or worse. Just like a Formula 1 team, a nonprofit will have a mix of data. Some of the data will be very objective, while some will be very subjective. Some risk data will have great urgency, while other risk data can be used for longer-term strategic decisions. Some data will be presented in a quick and easy-to-digest form, and some data will take a longer time to collect and digest.

The key point is that data is extremely useful, and this chapter outlines some of the key ideas of data analysis and management for effective nonprofit risk management.

Some Key Data Principles

Before beginning an analysis of the different data techniques, it is useful to take a look at some key data principles to always keep in mind. Our experience has been that data analysis can be very intimidating or confusing to many. The reality is that is does not need to be so. In fact, if the data analysis is confusing, then it likely means that the data analysis is being conducted incorrectly.

The first adage to keep in mind when doing data analysis is that "it is better to be approximately right than precisely wrong." While we obviously do not want to encourage sloppy data analysis, the point is that there is often little use obsessing about fine details. The point is to be consistent, practical, and unbiased in collecting and analyzing data.

Like all aspects of risk management, data analysis exists to provide value. If the costs to collect and analyze the data are more than the benefits it will bring, then one should really question why the data analysis is being done. While the quest for precision is admirable, there is a practical point at which one realizes that there are diminishing returns for the effort.

There is a process to risk data analysis. We break the process into five steps as illustrated in Figure 5.1: identify, measure, evaluate, prioritize, and then action. In our opinion, the most critical as well as the most valuable step is the first step: identifying the risks and identifying the data or metrics that will be used to analyze those risks. We prioritize the identification step as it is in line with our first law of risk management; the mere fact that you identify that a risk exists automatically improves your management of it.

Identifying risk and determining the appropriate way to measure the risk is not always a trivial task. It requires creativity, it requires an extensive knowledge of the operations of the organization, and it usually requires a fair bit of inspired foresight. It also requires a diversity of input, which is a point that is often missed or underappreciated.

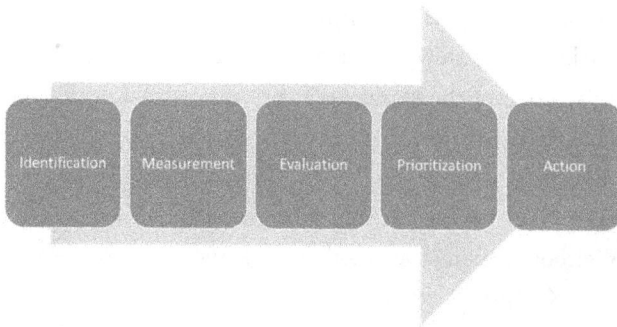

Figure 5.1 Data analysis process

Determining how to measure the risk often requires some creativity. The risk measures of a for-profit financial institution tend to be very quantitative and objective, for instance, what percentage of loans are delinquent and what are the sizes of the delinquent loans. Conversely, the risk measures for a nonprofit are often qualitative and subjective, such as are we improving the quality of lives of our beneficiaries. Coming up with risk metrics for such "fuzzy" queries is necessary but nontrivial. Again, a diversity of inputs is generally helpful.

Evaluation can be simple and basic, or it can be quite sophisticated. When deciding how to evaluate data, two questions should be kept in mind. The first question that the evaluation needs to answer is, "Are we getting better at managing this risk?" The second question that evaluation should answer is, "How can we get better at managing this risk?" A fantastic evaluation that does not aid in answering these two questions is simply an academic exercise.

The next step is to prioritize the data. Without prioritization it is quite possible to drown in data and get nothing done. Not all data is applicable, and not all data is applicable all of the time. It is useful to realize that the prioritization can take place at many stages. Some curation of data is likely to take place at the identification stage—although we caution about being too hasty in dismissing some types of data or risks as being irrelevant. It is a balancing act. The point is that data (and risks) need to be curated and prioritized in order for risk management to be an efficient process.

When prioritizing the data, it is wise to keep in mind business guru Peter Drucker's well-known statement, "What gets measured, gets managed." This is one of the reasons that prioritization is critical. It is also wise to realize that the corollary is generally also true; what doesn't get measured doesn't get managed.

The final, and next to identification, most important step is action. Analysis without action is yet another academic exercise. The action step is covered in Chapter 9, "Risk Treatment."

Eisenhower once stated that "in times of war, planning is indispensable, plans are useless." We believe that the same is true of risk analytics. The value of going through the risk process is often in the process itself. In going through the process, management (and the board and staff) gain useful insights into the working of the organization. When risk occurs (e.g., through accidents or random events), the actual risk data may not prove that useful, but the insights gained through completing the risk data process may prove to be of significant value.

A final principle is that the trend of the data is often more important and more telling than the actual values of the data itself. Risk is a process, and a dynamic one at that. Risk is not static. One organization that we are familiar with presents its quarterly risk summary to the board and to its stakeholders as a story with twists, turns, and surprises. This presentation as a story opens up questions about how future "chapters" may develop, which is very useful. Recall that a general principle of risk is that it is forward-looking. Data analysis can be used to understand the past but is most effective when used to contemplate how the future might develop. Recall the two questions that we posed earlier in this section: "Are we getting better at risk management?" and "How can we get better at risk management?" Ultimately this is the core of risk management and data analysis.

Risk Maps

A helpful place to start with risk identification is a risk map. A risk map plots the three main parameters of a risk: the level of impact (positive or negative), the probability of the risk, and the amount of control (actual or possible) that the organization may have over the risk. A sample risk map is shown in Figure 5.2.

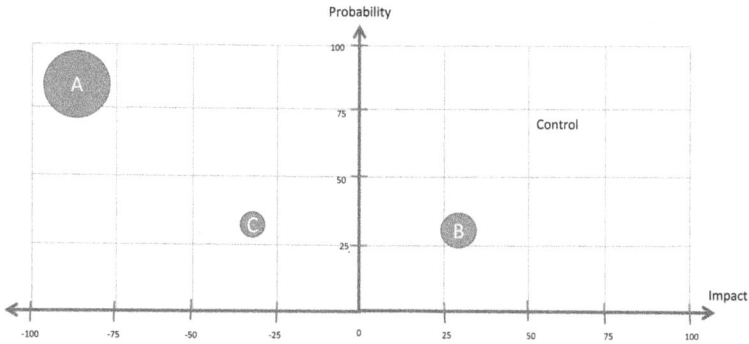

Figure 5.2 A sample risk map

In this simple risk map, there are two risks that are mapped. Risk A is a large negative-impact risk, which also has a relatively high probability of occurring. Conversely, Risk B is a positive risk, but it has a low impact and a low probability of occurring. In addition, the circle denoting Risk A is large, which indicates that it is a risk that the organization does not have a lot of control over or good risk management of. Risk B is shown with a small circle, which implies that the organization has a lot of control over or good risk management of.[1] Risk C is a negative risk, but it has little impact, a small probability of occurring, and the small circle it is drawn with shows that the organization is confident that it has control of this risk.

The risk map shows the risks that should be a priority for management. For instance, Risk A should be a priority for management over Risk C. Risk A has large negative impact, a high probability of occurring, and the organization believes it currently has little control over it. The organization should be developing a risk management plan to alter its assessment of Risk A so that it has a lower negative impact and a lower probability of occurring, and the organization is more confident that it has adequate control over the risk. Likewise, the organization may want to think of risk management techniques so as to increase the probability of Risk B occurring, and to increase its impact if it does occur. This would shift the plotting of Risk B further to the right and upward. These risk

---

[1] Note that some authors, and some organizations use the opposite convention for illustrating risk control in their risk maps. That is, some organizations have a small circle signifying limited control, and a large circle signifying a large amount of control.

management actions would hopefully make the revised risk map look more like that shown in Figure 5.3.

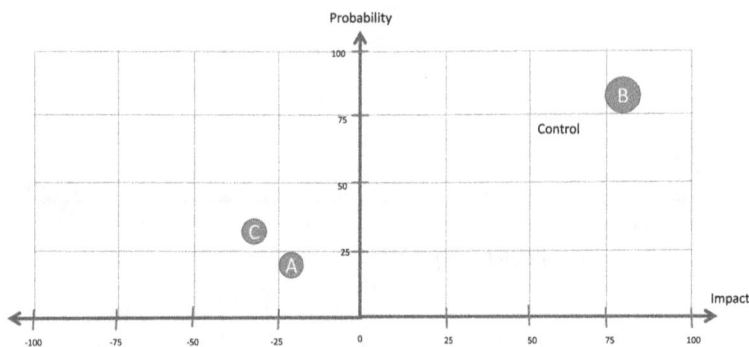

Figure 5.3 A risk map after suggested actions

A series of risk maps through time create a simple illustration of how well the organization is doing at managing its risks. The objective, of course, is to manage high negative-impact risks that have a high probability of occurring from Point 1 to Point 2 as shown in Figure 5.4, and, likewise, to manage positive risks that have low probability and low impact from Point 3 to Point 4. This is the essence of risk management illustrated by a risk map.

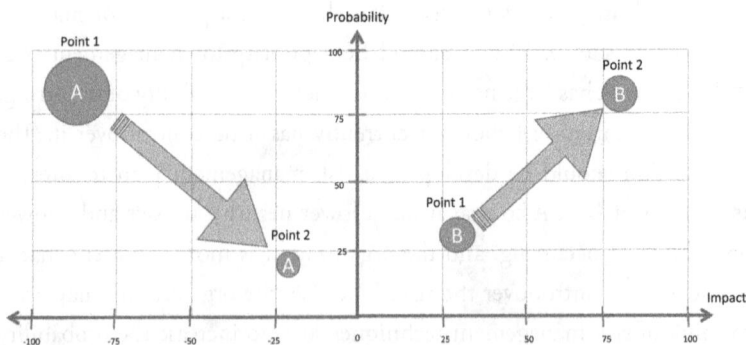

Figure 5.4 Risk management objectives illustrated by a risk map

Target placements on a risk map can be used to gauge how the organization is doing relative to its target for each risk. This is one way of assessing how the organization is achieving its risk management objectives, particularly when the progress toward the goal is tracked through time.

Identifying and Measuring Risks

The risk map is a simple concept; but how does one go about identifying the risks, assessing their impact and probability, as well as assessing the perceived level of control or risk management? This is obviously an important but nontrivial task.

The first method is to obviously have management or the board or the staff or some combination of the aforementioned develop the list of risks, as well as the assessment of impact, probability, and control of the risks. This is an obvious way to start the process but getting some form of agreement or consensus can be challenging. People will naturally have different ideas about what the most significant risks are and what their assessment of those risks are.

To avoid conflict, avoid bias, avoid the work required, and to outsource the task of risk identification and assessment, some organizations will turn to consultants for the task. Assigning the task to consultants has its advantages and disadvantages. Consultants, of course, have experience with a wide range of organizations, along with specialized risk expertise. However, if the job is "completely" outsourced, and if the consultants do not actively engage stakeholders of the nonprofit in their process, then there will be a lack of internal ownership in the risk management process. If management, staff, and the board are not fully engaged with the consultants in compiling the risk assessment, then not only an opportunity for ownership of the risks will be lost, but also a significant amount of risk learning that occurs during a risk assessment.[2]

One method that many organizations have found useful for risk identification and assessment is the Delphi Method. In the Delphi Method, a diverse group of stakeholders are assembled and led through a facilitated session. The first step is to develop a list of risks. This is generally done by getting participants to anonymously write a list of risks on a piece of paper and then the facilitator can compile the lists for the entire working group to view. A facilitated discussion of the risks can be run, and this discussion should be as neutral as possible. It is an opportunity for people to briefly comment on the list

---

[2]Note: As risk consultants, we have an obvious bias that you should take into account when reading this particular section on consultants.

that has been developed. Another round or two of listing additional risks is generally useful as seeing the original list will spark ideas in the participants.

The second stage of the Delphi Method is that the participants anonymously assess each of the risks for the three parameters of impact, probability and control. The process is again done anonymously to avoid bias, groupthink, and to avoid a dominant personality from taking control or intimidating the group. Once participants have submitted their assessments, the results are shown to the group and a facilitated discussion follows. This process, of anonymous assessment, display of results, and facilitated discussion is repeated until a consensus begins to form.

The Delphi Method has proven to be a very useful method for identifying and assessing risks, such as for the purpose of constructing a risk map. The two key and absolutely necessary elements are to involve a diverse group of participants, and to have anonymity in the process. It is important to have a group that is cognitively different (as opposed to identity diversity). Stakeholders in different functions of the organization and at different levels of the organization and with different academic and professional experience should be included. The cognitive diversity combined with the anonymity is what makes the process so useful and effective. The anonymity can be maintained by having paper votes, or by using voting machines that are quite commonly used in a variety of educational settings. There are even phone apps that can be used for the process that display results for the group automatically.

One element that needs to be communicated beforehand to the participants in a Delphi Method exercise is some definitions as to levels of each of the parameters being assessed. Many of the risks discussed will be quite subjective; thus, chaos can ensue if a set of common definitions is not adopted. For probability it is suggested that ranges of probability are used. Tables 5.1 and 5.2, respectively, show suggested definitions for probability and impact definitions. Of course, the organizations will want to adopt definitions and a level of granularity that are most useful for their own purposes. We somewhat arbitrarily picked five levels of granularity for illustrative purposes only.

Table 5.1 *Probability range definitions*

Assessment of Probability	Probability Range
Very Low	0 – 5%
Low	5 – 25%
Average	25 – 75%
High	75 – 95%
Very High	95 – 100%

Table 5.2 *Impact definitions*

Assessment of Impact	Description
Very Low	Barely perceptible
Low	Noticeable but does not require change in operations
Average	Noticeable and requires a small change in operations
High	Requires significant changes in operations
Very High	Has a dramatic impact on operations

Risk Dashboards

Let's briefly refer back to the Formula 1 race car comparison that we started this chapter with. The driver of the car obviously has a lot on their mind. They cannot be distracted with a flood of data coming at them that needs to be interpreted while they are trying to drive the car and pass other drivers. What the driver needs is a simple display in front of them only those variables that they absolutely need to function effectively. That display, of course, is a dashboard.

Just like a race car driver needs a dashboard, so too do different people in the organization need risk dashboards. Furthermore, different people, at different levels, will need different dashboards. A dashboard is a simple and clear to read minimal display of the basic and most necessary risk variables that immediate attention should be paid to. For instance, in your car your dashboard consists of a speedometer, a tachometer (if your car is a manual gear shift), a fuel level reading, and an oil temperature gauge. There is also likely a "Check Engine Soon" light that will come on if further analysis is warranted. While there is a whole host of other information available for the car driver (radio station, temperature, a clock, etc.), that information is almost always off to side as it is not necessary data for the safe operation of the vehicle.

We think a car dashboard is an excellent example to copy for a risk dashboard. There should be three or four main variables displayed in an easy to read fashion, as well as a "Check Engine" type of signal that indicates that further analysis of other issues is warranted. The key to developing a good risk dashboard is in determining the key variables to display, and how to display them. For instance, on your car's dashboard, only the vital and immediately necessary variables are displayed. Furthermore, a lot of thought goes into how the variables are displayed. For instance, the dial for oil pressure is easy to read, the normal operating range is clearly marked, and in addition a danger zone range is also clearly marked.

The key variables for the risk dashboards are those variables that answer the first of the two risk analytics questions that we posed earlier in this chapter, "Are we getting better at managing risk?" Determining what these key variables are requires some thought, but the process of determining the variables produces insight into the risk operations of the organization and thus is time and effort that is well invested.

As with the other methods, aspirations for each of the key metrics could be illustrated on the risk dashboard so an assessment can be made of the measure in question relative to its target value. Again, examples from your car's dashboard generally have some indication of normal operating range embedded on the dial as in, for instance, the normal operating range on your oil temperature gauge.

Different risk dashboards that are produced for different levels and functions of the operations are an efficient and effective way to keep risk in the focus of staff and stakeholders in a way that is easy, convenient, helpful, and unobtrusive.

Risk Radars

Using coordinate systems may be an effective way of illustrating the risks; however, there may be other practical ways as well. Another visual technique we propose to use for the risk management is called the risk radar. With similar logic as for risk maps, the risk radar can be used for departments, services or the risk types as illustrated in the following drawing.

The three parameters of risk are drawn separately which makes it easier for decision makers to see the big picture go in deep as much as they want. We can also add thresholds on the graph to have a managerial warning mechanism. Again, the models and tools we propose in this book are kept generic and flexible so that nonprofit organizations can customize them based on their specific needs (Figures 5.5 and 5.6).

As for the graphs, the risk radar can also be used for the strategic planning purposes. The following graphs illustrate three different strategic plans for three risk parameters: probability, impact, and the level of control. Since the risk radar is scaled between 0 and 100 (although again, the labels could be qualitative from very low to very high as we used previously), we may use color coding or a separate graph to indicate a risk with a desired impact (opportunity). Otherwise the scale between 0 and 100 represent the undesired level of impact of the risk.

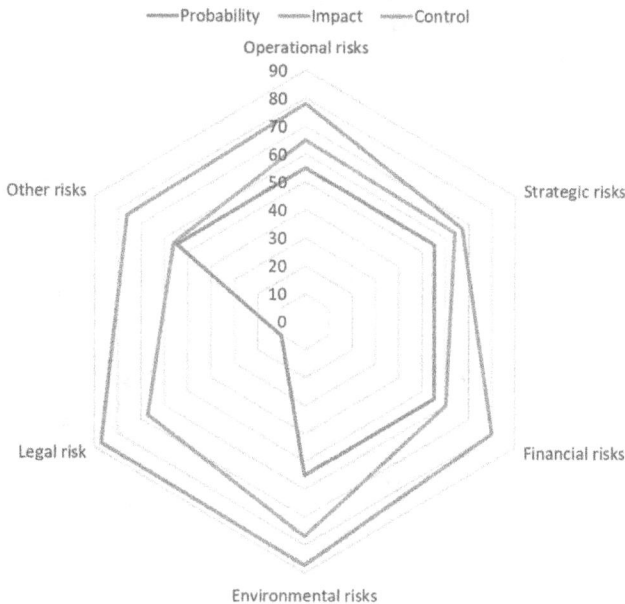

Figure 5.5 Risk radar

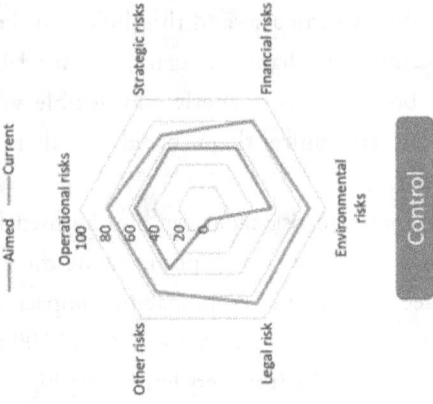

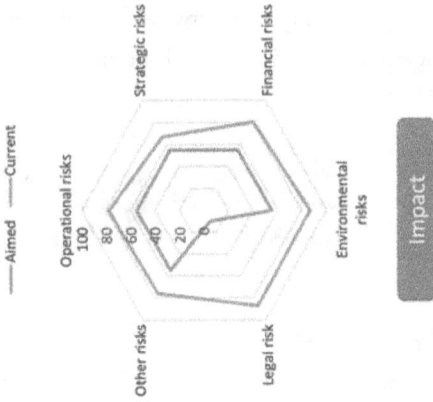

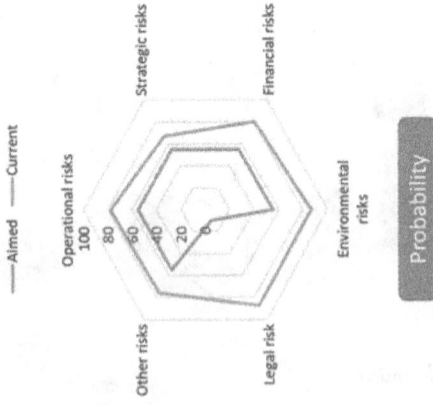

Figure 5.6 *Risk radars*

Risk Scenarios and Backcasting

Risks for whatever reason do not tend to occur in isolation. They tend to be correlated, or to occur in clumps. It is a version of the adage that "it never rains but it pours." For this reason, it is important to take this clumping or correlation of risks into account. This can be done by scenario analysis.

A scenario analysis is where an imagined confluence of risks is considered. Scenarios can be developed by management, by the board, or by working groups for the various units of the nonprofit. Developing scenarios helps in the development of contingency plans and facilitates discussion of "what-if?" management techniques. Scenario creation explicitly plays into our first law of risk management (the mere fact that you acknowledge a risk exists, automatically improves your management of that risk—or in the case of risk scenarios, it improves your management of the portfolio of risks.)

When developing risk scenarios there are two things to keep in mind. First off, the scenarios should be both positive and negative. If the focus is only on negative portfolio of risks, then those fortunate situations where a confluence of positive factors occur will be missed or not fully capitalized on. The second aspect is to consider best and worst plausible scenarios. Unrealistic risk scenarios may be fun or interesting (or scary) to consider but are not really productive exercises.

Managers probably are always implicitly doing scenario analysis in their heads; that is what makes them managers. However, there is value in expanding risk scenario workshops to a wider audience as it helps in the development of better scenarios and better risk plans. It also increases the risk awareness, and the risk learning of the organization as a whole. Finally, formalizing and making a record of the process greatly aids in the institutional risk knowledge of the organization.

A particular form of risk scenario is called backcasting or a premortem. In backcasting, you look forward 5 years (or whatever period of time that you are creating scenarios for) and you assume that the organization has missed its targets. You then create the scenarios that could have caused the targets to have been missed. As always, it is useful to assume that you underperformed or overperformed so as to capture scenarios of good risk as well as bad risk.

Risk Registers and Risk Evolution

A risk register is a catalog of the risks of the organization. It includes items such as a listing of the risks, the impact of the risk, how the organization dealt with the risks (or plans to deal with the risks), the costs of managing the various risks, the result or effectiveness of the risk management, the change in the level of risk after management, any contingency plans, and a host of other possible variables. Basically, a risk register is a risk history of the organization. It complements the activities that we have discussed in this chapter, including risk maps, risk dashboards, and risk radars.

Whatever the method used to record and manage risks, we believe that the important thing is how the organization is evolving in risk. A time series of the risk data can help in answering the question of "is the organization getting better at managing risk?" As risk cannot be conquered, the best that one can hope for is that they are getting better at managing the risk.

For instance, consider the evolution of the two risks that are illustrated in the risk map shown in Figure 5.7.

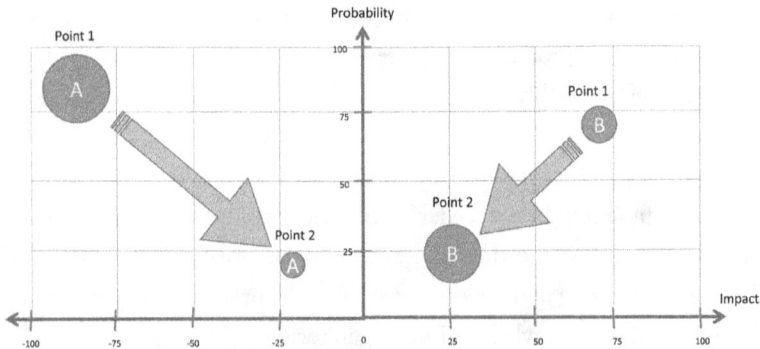

Figure 5.7 Evolution of risk

We see that Risk A has moved from being a high-probability and high-impact negative risk with little level of control, to be a risk with much lower impact, much less probability of occurring, and a significant amount of greater control. Conversely, Risk B, a positive risk, has moved from having medium impact, medium probability, and medium control to having a lower impact and with lower probability. The risk management for Risk A has improved dramatically, while the risk management of Risk B has actually made things worse!

Being aware of trends in the risks of an organization can tell a manager a lot about how well their risk management activities are actually performing.

Risk Scores

Before concluding this chapter, it is helpful to consider some quantification of the risk analysis. As mentioned earlier, many of the risks for a nonprofit will tend to be qualitative in nature. Developing a risk score is an attempt to try to put some level of quantification on the risks as an aid in prioritizing the risks in a systematic fashion. We will be the first to admit that this is not always trivial to do, and we warn against being too zealous in attempting to do so.

One way to adapt a risk score is to start by referring back to Tables 5.1 and 5.2 where we put definitions on risks that were qualitatively ranked from very low to very high in terms of their probabilities and their impacts. Very low risks could be given a score of 1, low risks a score of 2, and so forth with a very high risk being given a score of 5. Negative risks could be given a negative number in addition to signify that there is a significant difference between a very high positive risk and a very high negative risk.

Sometimes, when risks are ranked this way the score for the probability can be multiplied by the score for the impact to give an overall score. To add in the effect of the control factor of the risk, the multiplied value of the probability and the impact can be divided by the score for the amount of control, with high control being given a score of 5, and a low amount of control being given a score of 1. When multiplying, it is, of course, important to keep in mind that the overall score of a negative risk should ultimately remain negative (and thus ignore the fact that multiplying two negative numbers produces a positive answer).

Risk scores are not a perfect way to objectively rank risks. For instance, a low probability of occurrence does not always balance out a high impact. For this reason, we suggest that the final ranked list be judgmentally checked for reasonableness.

Concluding Thoughts

Identifying and assessing risks is a tricky yet necessary task for risk management. You cannot manage risks unless you know what the risks are, what your current position is in terms of management, and some objectives in terms of where you want to be in terms of risk management. Furthermore, you cannot track the effectiveness of your risk management activities unless you have a record of how the risks and their associated variables are changing through time and due to risk management activities.

In this chapter we have attempted to give a process for analyzing risks and some tools and tactics for doing so. Admittedly it, like much of risk management, is as much of an art as it is a science. Remember that it is better to be approximately right than precisely wrong. It is also much better to be approximately right than completely ignorant of the risks.

The process of going through a risk analysis exercise on a periodic basis is of value, almost as much value of the outcomes of the risk analysis process itself. Attempting to perform even a somewhat imperfect analysis gives understanding of the risks and points to possibilities for managing.

Ultimately performing a risk analysis is an essential part of any effective risk management plan.

CHAPTER 6

Financial Risks

Virtually every nonprofit faces financial risks as well as financial stress.[1] More specifically almost every nonprofit faces difficulty or constraints in raising the funds required in order to achieve their goals and objectives. Generally, financial risk for a nonprofit is a negative risk, or a one-way risk. Rarely is the risk that the nonprofit has too much in the way of financial resources. Ironically, when this pleasant surprise does occur it likely might be a curse in disguise as feuds about how to spend the windfall may arise as new priorities become possible.

By definition, a nonprofit firm is not designed to operate at a profit, nor is it set-up to hoard excess financial resources for a future need. Thus, financial risk management is an ongoing activity for a nonprofit.

Financial data analysis is a whole field of study itself and could fill an entire book on its own (and many have been written). Many of the techniques are extreme and while useful for large organizations with plenty of historical data, and a team of experts to analyze the data, many of the techniques would be valueless overkill for many nonprofits. As with all analysis, there is a need for common sense and to avoid overkill.

In this chapter we discuss some methods for forecasting the needs and wants of the organization and the uncertainty in the sources of funding. We will also discuss some of the operating financial concerns and the need to balance the operational risk with the scale of the financing risk.

---

[1]Technically financial stress is a shortage of funds, while financial risk is the variability of cash flows or financing.

Forecasting Uncertainty

Risk management as previously stated is about the future. Forecasting the financial needs and resources is thus one of the pivotal tasks of risk management for a nonprofit firm.

Many nonprofits do a cursory job of forecasting needs, and an even more superficial job of forecasting resources, yet for many nonprofits this is sufficient. Essentially these organizations do little more than take the previous year's expenditures and expenses, perhaps adjust for inflation and then build their forecast off this.

For organizations that are mature and have a stable stakeholder base and a stable set of activities, this simplistic forecasting model is probably about as accurate as one might reasonably aspire to. Even in such stable situations, however, the organization might want to do some risk analysis.

The simplest analysis is to check the variability of previous year's results, and assuming that previous results are indicative of future results (not always a great assumption), some simple yet useful risk analysis can be done.

When looking at historical results, there are a few considerations to keep in mind. Depending on the scope of the operations, the first consideration is the timing. If the organization has large swings in cash inflows and inflows throughout the year, then there may be a requirement to do more frequent analysis on a quarterly or even monthly analysis. However, many organizations will simply examine their results on an annual basis.

A second aspect to keep in mind when looking at historical results is extraordinary values. For instance, the organization may have received an unusually large donation through the estate of a deceased benefactor. It has to be questioned if such a cash inflow is reasonable to include in the calculations for risk analysis purposes and for cash flow forecasting.[2] Such an extraordinary income for most nonprofits is uncertain, and thus a risk. However, it might reasonably be considered a case of a black swan event. A black swan event is a low probability event with a large impact.

---

[2]It is interesting to note that some organizations rely on one-time bequests from the estates of their benefactors. For instance, many faith-based organizations have built planned giving upon death into their financial projections. While a beneficial short-term solution, relying on the death of your constituents is obviously not a great long-term strategy.

Black swan events pose a challenge for risk management. They obviously occur, and by definition, they are significant. Furthermore, they are both significant on the upside (as in the example of a donation from the trust of a benefactor) and on the downside (such as a freak accident that leads to a crippling lawsuit). Black swan events can exaggerate the risk calculations leading to imprudent risk decisions. Eliminating them from the analysis, however, means that their effect is not incorporated.

One way of managing black swan events into the data is to examine an interquartile, or an interdecile range. To calculate the interdecile range, the historical data is ranked from best to worst outcome. After that is done, the top 10 percent of results are ignored, and likewise, the bottom 10 percent of results are ignored when doing further analysis. This eliminates the black swan data from analysis. This is a common technique to use when there may be extraordinary events that would otherwise skew the data for later analysis. The interquartile range is conducted in a similar fashion; only instead, the top 25 percent of results are eliminated, and the bottom 25 percent of the results are eliminated before conducting any analysis.

When looking at historical numbers, one can examine the absolute level of the values, or one can examine the growth on either a nominal or an inflation adjusted basis. Unless one is operating in a country (or a time) of high inflation, examining the nominal numbers is generally sufficient. The question of looking at the growth, or the absolute numbers is generally a more serious question.

Looking at the absolute numbers is easier as there are no calculations to be made. However, a lot of useful risk information is hidden in the absolute numbers. Taking the trouble to calculate the period to period growth can more easily illustrate trends or changes in growth patterns. For instance, the absolute numbers may be growing, while the growth trend is slowing significantly, or perhaps even falling.

Another useful analysis is to illustrate historical ratios. For instance, consider the case of a Little-League Baseball. Basing the historical number based on the number of participants shows trends in costs and revenues that are likely much more meaningful and telling than simply relying on the absolute historical analysis. If the data is available in a spreadsheet format, then such analysis is relatively easy and quick to complete.

Both growth rates and ratio analysis make it much more meaningful to look at the uncertainty of historical values as a guide to the level of future risk. Generally, the extra work mathematically is worth it in terms of the understanding of the numbers and the risk that it produces.

Variability is the key risk indicator. The greater the variability, the greater the risk. Measurement of historical and future variability can be quite sophisticated. Such sophistication is generally not warranted for nonprofits, so we will focus on a few basic elements. The most basic variability measure is the range. The range looks at the highs and lows in the past numbers. This is generally meaningless when looking at absolute numbers, but when looking at growth rates it can be quite telling. Figure 6.1 looks at the historical expenses for two fictional organizations. Both organizations have the same long-term growth rate of expenses, and they both started and ended the 10-year period with expenses of 100 and 250 respectively. However, the range of Organization A's expenses is much greater than the range of the growth of Organization's B expenses. Thus, it is obvious that Organization A has more financial risk in its expenses than Organization B.[3]

A more refined calculation of variability than the range is standard deviation. Standard deviation is a common measure of risk that is used in a

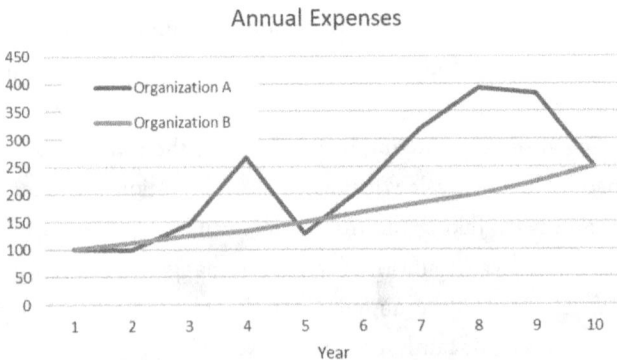

Figure 6.1 Financial Variability

---

[3]Observers will note that there is a strong trend in the expenses of both organizations in the example. For a more complete and accurate analysis one should use detrending techniques. Detrending techniques are beyond the scope of this book and generally are not needed for most nonprofits with typical risk management analysis needs.

variety of applications. Calculation of standard deviation is also built into most spreadsheet programs. Standard deviation calculates the deviations around a mean value. Although standard deviation is more complicated than variability, it is quite useful for risk management. For instance, if we know the mean of a set of values, and if we know the standard deviation of that series of values then we know that roughly 2/3rds of the values will lie within plus one or minus one standard deviation of the mean. Likewise, approximately 95 percent of all values will lie between plus or minus two standard deviations of the mean.

For instance, in the above example for Organization A and Organization B, the mean growth in annual expenses was 20 percent and 11 percent, respectively. However, the standard deviation for Organization A was 46 percent, but for Organization B it was only 2 percent. Based on this information we can state that approximately 2/3rds of the time the annual growth of expenses for Organization A will be between a negative 26 percent and a positive 66 percent, while for Organization B, the annual growth in expenses will be between 9 percent and 13 percent. Organization A obviously has a much greater variability in its expense growth and thus much more financial risk.

While on the subject of standard deviation, and referring back to the discussion on whether or not to include black swan event data into any data analysis, we should note that it is common to exclude any data that it more than two standard deviations away from the average. This is a more refined technique than using the interdecile or the interquartile range method that was mentioned in the previous section. Admittedly though, this likely falls into the category of overkill in analysis for most nonprofits.

Variability, and particularly standard deviation are powerful aids in risk planning and management. Knowing what the range of outcomes is likely to be helps immensely in making sure that objectives and goals are accomplished.

Scenario Analysis and Stress Analysis

Using the range, and preferably the standard deviation, for the major elements in both the resources and uses of funds budget will greatly aid in showing where surpluses and shortfalls are likely to occur. One technique for doing so is to use standard deviation (or similarly the range) to look at what the forecasts would be with a one or two standard deviation move. For instance, the budget could be made assuming a one standard deviation increase of expenses and a one standard deviation fall in revenues. This would comprise one way of devising a reasonable worst-case scenario. (Indeed, it would be a severe worst-case scenario.) Likewise, a positive best-case scenario could be developed assuming that the revenue sources all experienced a one standard deviation increase in their growth rates while the expenses experienced a one standard deviation fall in their growth rates. Repeating the experience with a two standard deviation move would comprise an extreme worst case and extreme best case set of scenarios.

Scenario Analysis is a key technique in risk analysis. The one and two standard deviation method described in one way to develop a scenario analysis. As the name implies, though, another way is to develop a set of events that might happen to the organization and develop the financial plans based on these scenarios. Again, it is useful to develop both positive and negative scenarios. The trick is to keep a balanced measure on the scenarios; one does not just want to create overly rosy projections, nor does one want to only create unwarranted depressingly gloomy projections.

Scenario analysis is not only useful for the numbers that it provides to guide risk management but also useful as a process. Scenario analysis is basically an exercise in assuming that the financial projections will be missed and then backtracking to come up with reasonable scenarios as to how and why such a miss in projections might occur. There is significant value in asking that question and developing scenarios. (Remember the first law of risk management: the mere fact that you acknowledge that the risk exists automatically improves your ability to manage it.)

Five-Year Financial Risk

Every organization, for-profit, or nonprofit should make some type of forward projections, and a 5-year forward projection is common. This may seem to be a bit of a stretch for many nonprofits given to their tendency of relatively rapid changeover of board members, staff, and volunteers. This is particularly true for nonprofits that are involved in youth activities, as the staff and volunteers only think in terms of their involvement when their children are involved—which, of course, they likely will not be in 5 years' time.

Looking forward for a significant period of time, however, is useful for several reasons.[4] For starters, the capital budgeting projects of the organization will have significant effects beyond the next year's budget cycle. There needs to be a balance between managing for the present and the near future, and the long-term success of the organization. This is particularly true for a financially constrained nonprofit. It has significant spill-over implications for the risk management of the organization.

Another reason is what we call the 5-year risk exercise that was previously discussed. The 5-year exercise consists of looking forward 5 years and listing reasons why the organization failed to achieve its objectives and forecasts. (Again, missing the objectives and forecasts could be underachieving or overachieving.) As previously discussed, the point of the exercise is to create the risk scenarios to which the organization might be exposed. It works for not only operational and strategic risk but also for financial risk.

Burn Rate

There is a financial variable that is often used by entrepreneurial firms that also has applicability for those nonprofits that rely upon benefactors or grants for their survival (as opposed to cost recovery fee for service nonprofits). The burn rate is the number of days that an organization can go without any cash inflows. In the case of a for-profit firm, it is the number of days it can go without making a sale. It is basically the cash on hand divided by the average daily expenses. Start-up firms (and their investors) closely watch the burn rate as it is a measure of how much risk there is in the development of the firm. It gives a measure of how long the company has to develop their product before they go bankrupt.

The reason to calculate the burn rate for a nonprofit is somewhat different. For those nonprofits that rely on benefactors to cover their

---

[4]There is nothing particularly magic about 5 years. The time period being forecasted could just as well be 3 years. The point is to look beyond the next year's planning cycle.

operating expenses, the burn rate gives the expected life of the organization until it needs to find a new set of benefactors. In essence, the burn rate is an urgency indicator.

In general, the greater the variability of the expenses, the greater the number of days should be that the organization can survive without new cash inflows from benefactors. The burn rate is a key indicator for the desired minimum cash balance of the firm, which will be discussed in the working capital management section.

Capital Budgeting

The previous section introduced the concept of variability as something that should be developed into the planning and budgeting for the organization. In this section and the next we will examine the two most important parts of the financial planning exercise; the capital budget and the cash budget. The capital budget lays out the long-term expenditures for the organization. These are extraordinary expenses, or income producing events such as fundraising campaigns, that occur as nonrecurring or at infrequent periods. For example, spending money to build a new facility would be an example of a capital budgeting plan, while ongoing maintenance expenses would be part of the cash budget, which is also sometimes called the operating budget.

Capital budget items tend to be long-term items that are critically important to the long-term mission of the organization. Thus, capital budget items are key risk variables. They have high uncertainty due to their long-term time frame, and they have high impact, due to their longevity.

Capital budgeting activities can be broken up into "nice-to-do" and "must-do." The must-do items are, as the name implies, those items that must be completed with a certain period of time. They are key to the organization and its mission. Without this item being completed, the organization has no reason for continuing or cannot continue. The only flexibility may be some potential variability in the timing of the expenditure or event. The must-do capital budget items are obviously at the center of any budgeting exercise. Furthermore, they should be incorporated into the budgeting exercise as soon as they become known. The sooner they are incorporated into the budgeting exercise, the more advantage can be taken of any timing flexibility that might occur.

Discretionary capital budget items might include items such as building a new ball field for a Little-League nonprofit, or purchasing new band equipment for a music group, or perhaps building renovations to allow expansion for a second language program for new immigrants. One item that is frequently forgotten is that capital budget items generally also change the operating budget in that new capital resources generally (but not always) require increases in ongoing operating expenses. They may also require new nonmonetary resources such as extra volunteers, or a larger time commitment on existing staff.

Capital budget expenses also tend to be underestimated, or equivalently overly optimistic in their financial projections. Unfortunately, projects of all types rarely come in on budget and on time, and major capital expenditures are no exception. Allowances should be made for such overly optimistic projections.

In for-profit companies, capital budgeting is a value-based exercise in which the projected cash flows are discounted back at the cost of capital (essentially the borrowing costs of the firm) to see whether or not the proposed project will enhance the value of the company. This is not really a relevant exercise for a nonprofit as their projects are not intended to increase the financial wealth of the stakeholders. Of course, nonprofits add value to their beneficiaries in other ways that cannot be measured by wealth.

Working Capital Management

Working capital is also called operating capital. It is the cash flows that fund the day to day operating activities of the organization. Working capital is rightly the focus of attention when it comes to budgeting for nonprofits. It should also be the focus for risk management.

Accurate assessment of working capital and in forecasting future budgets is key. An inaccurate forecast means that the organization could run out of money and thus have to close or curtail activities. Conversely, an inaccurate forecast may lead to the organization limiting their activities in order to conserve cash only to realize that they did have the available funds that would have allowed them to pursue additional activities and thus enhance their services to their beneficiaries.

As with other aspects of financial risks, looking at the variability in past forecasts (budgets) gives a clue to the level of variability or risk. It also really helps if there is someone who is familiar with the construction of the numbers (that is the forecasts and the budgets) who has a long history with the organization. A person with the knowledge and the history, brings a level of institutional historical knowledge as to why previous budgets either made or missed their forecasts. This is valuable information for risk analysis.

Unfortunately, few institutions will be so lucky to have someone with the characteristics of a long history with the financials. Ironically, and this is particularly true if the treasurer's role is a volunteer one, the role turns over on a frequent basis due to its demands. Being treasurer of any organization requires a unique set of skills, and can involve a fair bit of rather boring detail work that is generally far removed from what be considered the more interesting or satisfying roles to play in a nonprofit. It can also involve a fair bit of stress as there are many details to keep track of as well as a variety of people asking questions about funds for their respective area. For these reasons turnover in the treasurer's role tends to be high.

To account for this fact, but yet still in an effort to keep a record of budgeting misses, the board of the nonprofit should schedule an annual budget recap meeting, just like they schedule an annual budgeting meeting. The purposes of the recap meeting is to discuss, and record, the reasons why the various budgetary forecasts turned out to be inaccurate. Doing so will provide a valuable aid in assessing budgeting risk, but also in improving future budget forecasts. It will also help in strategic funding by indicating when a major capital funding campaign might be needed.

It is important to note that the purpose of the budget recap meeting is not to assign blame; it is to learn about the risks of budgeting for the organization. The only reason that a budget forecast will be on target is by a fluke. Forecasts are not certainty. Forecasts involve uncertainty and risk and thus there will be deviations. The budget recap meeting is to help to better understand how and why those deviations arise, and to try to discover if there is a way to better manage such deviations.

Funding Risk

Funding risk is the variability of the cash inflows from the sponsors of the organization. While working capital risk looks at the variability of the outgoing cash flows, funding risk examines the variability of the incoming cash flows.

Nonprofits rely upon a mixture of funding sources, each of which have their own levels of size, uncertainty, and variability. Sponsors such as donors or grant agencies can be particularly uncertain. There is a tendency for nonprofits to focus on the largest on the potential sponsors such as the major granting agencies, but this can lead to increasing risk due to the tight competition for grants from these agencies and other large donors. Former poker player, and a nonprofit board member, Annie Duke recommends that nonprofits should focus on the expected value of the source of funds in determining the risk and where the organization should focus their efforts. She relates her experience as a board member and consultant to After-School All Stars Organization, which provides after-school programming to underserved youth.[5] The organization, like most nonprofits, was focusing their efforts on the largest potential grants that they might be eligible for. However, this provided a distorted sense of the expected value and represented misplaced effort.

Consider, for instance, a $1,000,000 grant that the organization believed it had a 5 percent chance of winning. It would have an expected value of $50,000. Conversely, a potential donor, may be considering a $250,000 donation, which the organization believes it has a 50 percent chance of securing. This donation has an expected value of $125,000. Although the donation had a quarter of the potential value of the grant, the expected value was more than twice that of the grant after the probability of actually obtaining the monies was factored in.

Considering the probability of the funding source, in addition to the size of the potential funding, gives a much better picture of the actual risk involved. It is a better guide to the allocation of resources in attempting to secure the funds, but it is also a much better guide for the risk management of the funding task.

---

[5]A. Duke. 2018. *Thinking in Bets: Making Smarter Decisions When You Don't Have All the Facts* (New York, NY: Portfolio).

One important aspect of fundraising risk is unfortunately out of control of the organization and that is the risk of the general economy. When the economy is suffering there is a corresponding decrease in the willingness or the ability of potential donors to support the organization. This sometimes becomes a double effect as the need for the services of the nonprofits will also correspondingly increase—for example the services of food banks that are correlated with the general state of the economy.

A related aspect is government regulations in how donations are treated for tax purposes. For example, consider the plight of Feed Our Babies, a Phoenix-based charity that works to provide meals to low-income children in the area. A change in the standard tax deduction in 2018, while saving tax-payers money, also reduced the incentive for charitable giving. Feed Our Babies as a result saw tax-deductible donations from individuals fall by more than half.[6]

Economic events that affect fundraising can be national in scope or even local in scope. A general trend that seems to be developing is that young millennials are less likely to make charitable donations. In part, many believe this is due to their diminished economic prospects and high level of debt. The flip side is that the anecdotal evidence is that although their ability to donate may be compromised, their willingness to volunteer may be greater than for other demographic groups. Relatedly, as the baby-boomers start retiring in record numbers, there will likely be an increase in their willingness to volunteer their time to nonprofits.

Balancing Operating and Funding Risk

As a general rule, the greater the funding risk, the smaller the financial operating risk should be. This is particularly true if the organization has a particularly high burn rate. In essence this implies that the greater the funding uncertainty, the lower the uncertainty should be in the operating budget. If funding risk is unduly high, it may be necessary for the organization to be much more conservative in their operational plans than they

---

[6]Guest Opinion. May 21, 2019. "New Tax Law Triggers Fewer Donations to Nonprofits," *Arizona Capital Times*. https://azcapitoltimes.com/news/2019/05/21/new-tax-law-triggers-fewer-donations-to-nonprofits/ (accessed November 20, 2019).

would be otherwise. This may involve delaying projects, or cutting back on services offered to increase the likelihood that expenses will be covered.

If funding risk is high, the organization needs to face the difficult choice of whether it is better to cut or curtail some services, or chance having the organization go out of operation altogether due to exhaustion of financing. This is the reality for many nonprofits who do not monitor their net financial risk.

Another factor that comes into play is the cash balance. The organization should have a preset cash balance that it tries to maintain. The cash balance is a rainy-day fund so to speak. It is a buffer for when expenses are greater than expected or inflows are less than expected. Setting the cash balance is a balancing act between the variability of cash inflows and outflows, the burn rate of the organization and the level of risk regarding the suspension of services that that the organization is willing to accept.

Concluding Thoughts

The reality of most nonprofits is that they are cash constrained. Additionally, they generally have limited scope to change the cash inflows that they use to fund their operations. For this reason, management of the financing risks is particularly acute for nonprofits.

The task of risk management for the financing is to have a handle on the level of the financial risk, and to plan accordingly. Funding cycles tend to be long term in nature, while expenses tend to be more immediate. Financial risk management is thus an exercise in understanding the current position and forecasting the uncertainty in likely financial positions in the future.

Financial forecasting is not particularly easy to do, but conversely it is also not particularly difficult. In this chapter we have provided several simple measures and techniques for determining the level of risk, and for analyzing the level of risk going forward.

CHAPTER 7

Operational Risks

If a delicious dinner in a restaurant were "the strategy," then everything that is happening in the kitchen would be "the operation." Unfortunately, most of the stakeholders and society focus only on the strategic outcomes of nonprofit organizations. They rarely pay attention to what is happening in the kitchen.

The fact that operational risks are happening in the kitchen makes them less visible but not less important. We cannot talk about successful risk management in nonprofit organizations unless we pay enough attention to all types of risks including operational risks.

Operational risks are risks arising from people, infrastructure, and processes in place at the organization. More simply, it is risks arising from activities of the organization and those who perform those activities.

We have emphasized multiple times in this book that the risk is mostly about people. At the operational level, the involvement of human factor in risk is even more. The successful management of human resources in nonprofit organizations will mitigate the bad risk and create surprising opportunities at the operational level.

Nonprofits, in particular, tend to be focused on interactions of people. There generally are no large manufacturing plants involved in a nonprofit. Operations are what the people of the organization are doing for the benefit of other people. This brings people risk to the fore for nonprofits. For example, an inspiring interaction between an employee and a celebrity, who may become a major contributor as a volunteer or a generous donor, happens at the operational level but can change the overall status of the nonprofit in one day. An incident at the operational level may also have outcomes at the strategic level. In this way, the daily frontline interactions may have more impact than million-dollar marketing campaigns. For operational risk, even though processes are important, the focus should be on people.

Operational Processes

Most of the interactions between nonprofits and beneficiaries happen at the operational level. In addition, the density of human interactions during service provision creates unique potential areas of risk. Combined with the fact that nonprofits generally operate with a mix of professional employees and volunteer staff, it creates a combination that explains exactly why nonprofit organizations need better risk management tools and practices at the operational level.

The operational level is where the management plans and the decisions in nonprofit organizations are implemented. No matter how much the nonprofit organizations succeed in their planning and decision phases, their real performance depends on the successful implementation of those plans. This is where processes come into play. We can mitigate many internal or external interaction-related risks by well-defined operational processes. If all staff members and volunteers implement processes properly, the chances of having any problems will decrease.

The design of processes obviously begins with the strategic mission in mind. However, in addition to achieving strategic efficiency, the processes of the organization should also reflect good risk management. Just as processes should be periodically reviewed for their operational efficiency, so they should be reviewed for their risk efficiency. It is very easy to get into a routine when it comes to operational processes. "We have always done it this way," is not a reasonable justification for a process.

Well-honed processes have a lot of value. They allow for learning, which, in turn, leads to efficiency, they allow for new staffers and new volunteers to quickly get up to speed, they negate the need for recreating the wheel and thus allow time for performing the necessary activity rather than continually needing to rediscover how to do the activity, and they allow for consistency, which benefits all stakeholders. Processes also prevent people from doing stupid things, or performing ill-advised activities or performing normal activities in a dangerous manner. However, as discussed in Chapter 2, and in the story of Tomas Lopez (the lifeguard who did not follow the process for rescuing people who were swimming outside of the designated area), a process needs to be tempered with judgment.

For operations that are complicated, in that they follow rigid laws, a relatively strict adherence to a well-specified protocol or process is called for. For instance, this would apply to safety specifications, or regulations, such as food preparation regulations for a kitchen for the homeless.

For more complex situations, as in being a lifeguard, there will likely need to be a greater reliance of judgment. As previously discussed, situations regarding complex situations cannot be reduced to a set of rules, regulations, or best practice. This is where the experience, training, and intuition of the organization and its staff comes into play. You cannot write a rule book or a process book for complexity. The best you can rely on is guidebooks. This is why we previously stressed the importance of understanding the difference between complicated and complex situations.

When preparing operational risk management, it is very useful to separate risks into those that are complicated and those that are complex. Operations that are considered high risks that need to be managed, and that are also complex risks, are ones that the organization should endeavor to assign to the most capable and experienced staffers, as those are the risks that cannot be "codified" to a rigid operational process.

One way to ensure that processes are allowing for good risk management is to keep a risk history or a risk register as discussed in Chapter 5. When risks occur (again, both good and bad) an analysis should be done to find out if the process employed was a factor. Of course, this is simply good management practice, but a focus on risk management will help to bring in explicitly the risk factor, which is often overshadowed by strategic factors.

In addition to a risk history, it is also good practice to use the backcasting or premortem exercises that have been discussed in Chapter 5. Thinking about how a process may not work as intended is just as valuable as trying to forecast which process will work best. By nature, people tend to be optimistic and believe that their ideas will work as intended. However, research shows that there is significant value in being both optimistic and pessimistic when designing process. Backcasting or premortem exercises lead to synergistic improvements in processes both in terms of their efficiency and in terms of providing better risk management.

Human Capital Risk

Human capital is one of the most sensitive areas of risk in nonprofit organizations. Unlike a for-profit firm, nonprofits generally cannot rely on superior technology, proprietary knowledge, or better manufacturing processes as a comparative advantage or as a means to cover up poor people performance. Additionally, nonprofits by their nature tend to operate as service industries, which implies a lot of human-to-human interactions. Nonprofits are generally defined by the people they have as staff and volunteers, and the service that these people provide. As such, human capital is the most central ingredient to the success of the organization and thus necessarily the central risk.

Nonprofit organizations can benefit from staff members and volunteers as part of the solution to mitigate operational risks or just the opposite. It depends on the successful integration and involvement of staff in risk management at the operational level. Unfortunately, for many nonprofit organizations, attracting and retaining skilled employees is an ongoing challenge. The turnover rate tends to be higher than for those in for-profit industries or for those that work for government.

Operational performance is related not only with the staff members who deliver operations but also with those that manage the nonprofit or set the strategy. Managers should be selected not only for their dedication or commitment for the mission but also for their actual managerial abilities. Too frequently we have observed committed managers of nonprofits fail due to sufficient managerial experience or abilities. Passion is a wonderful motivator, but management is a set of attributes and skills that are not necessarily correlated with passion or specific technical skills. This is particularly true when it comes to the ability to manage risk.

Another important area of human capital risk is the board of directors. The composition of the board is key not only for strategic purposes but also for risk management purposes, a concept that will be discussed in Chapter 11 on governance.

In smaller charities, employees or volunteers who deliver very specific services or technical services become critical personnel. If they leave, it can dramatically affect the organization. We observed in several cases how human resources-related operational risks could become a major problem (or opportunity) in nonprofit organizations. For example, in a charity that offers services for deaf youth, the impact of the instructors was critical. They were not deaf themselves but knew sign language. They were critical to building a bridge between the charity and the deaf youth it served. It was a challenge to find instructors with signing expertise, especially given the unattractive compensation plans that the nonprofit was capable of providing.

Not surprisingly, compensation plans are not the primary reason for people to work at nonprofit organizations. They are nice people and do care about society. They usually share the social cause of their nonprofit organization and want to add value by playing a part.

This sincere and internal motivation of employees is very important in nonprofit organizations but may not last forever. It must be supported by external motivation, which simply may be a recognition. Sharing the cause of the charity is generally more important than the salary they get.

Human capital risks are tricky to manage. Contingency plans for key personnel should be developed, and slack in human capital resources should be developed as resources permit. Not only is it a risk to have key personnel leave the organization, but it can be an equal, or perhaps a bigger, negative risk to have them become burned out or stressed out.

Infrastructure Risk

Infrastructure is mainly composed of those parts of operations that we take for granted. Infrastructure is supply chains, any buildings and equipment of the organization, payments and receivables systems, stakeholder databases, any inventory, and of course, it also includes the information technology (IT) of the firm. The infrastructure forms the bones of any organization. In our terminology, infrastructure is basically the operational risks that do not involve people or processes.

Most (but not all) infrastructure risks tend to be relatively straightforward to deal with. The important thing is to recognize that risks exist. Most infrastructure risks also tend to be negative risks, although unexploited opportunities may exist that should be discovered. Infrastructure risks also tend to be simple or complicated risks rather than the trickier-to-deal-with complex risks.

Insurance policies are how many infrastructure risks are dealt with (e.g., buildings and equipment). Insurance, however, can at best compensate for discontinuity and is not a direct risk mitigant against service disruption. Here again a distinction can be made between for-profit and nonprofit organizations. If a for-profit firm loses sales as a result of a discontinuity risk in its infrastructure, an insurance payout for discontinuity will essentially make the company whole, with the possible exception of some lost customer goodwill. If a kitchen for the homeless suffers a discontinuity, then no compensation will make up for the fact that the beneficiaries of the nonprofit will potentially suffer from starvation. By definition, insurance compensation does not adequately hedge the activities of many nonprofits.

Obviously, minimizing the infrastructure is the first place to start. However, building redundancies and resilience into infrastructure is also required. For the major services, contingency plans are a must. This is yet another example of how building a comprehensive risk map helps to guide the nonprofit in their risk management activities. Having to cancel a week's worth of peewee baseball games due to a flood making a field unplayable has a very different impact than a flood forcing the closing of a homeless shelter. A simple example such as this brings home the importance of appreciating "impact" in risk mapping.

Increasingly, IT is a major part of an organization's infrastructure. It is an area of risk that the organization may be very aware of or very unaware of. Regardless of the degree of awareness, it is likely that IT is critical to a successful operation. A full discussion of IT risk is beyond the scope of this book. In any case, technology is changing at such a fast pace, that any specifics that we might discuss would be out of date before you, the reader, had a chance to purchase and read this book. Despite that, technology in terms of computer systems, social media, and accounts payable and receivable systems is critical.

For instance, IT inadequacy was a critical factor even for such a venerable institution as the Red Cross. In 2005, "Hurricane Katrina" destroyed huge parts of New Orleans, Louisiana, Mississippi, and Alabama. In all, Hurricane Katrina killed nearly 2,000 people and affected some 90,000 square miles of the United States.[1] When the disaster struck, U.S. officials

---

[1] https://www.history.com/topics/natural-disasters-and-environment/hurricane-katrina (accessed July 22, 2019).

addressed the Red Cross as the only charity. However, the Red Cross was not ready to respond to such a big catastrophe. Soon after Katrina, the CEO of the American Red Cross resigned amid criticism of the charity's disaster relief efforts. Many politicians and society members questioned placing such great responsibility in the hands of one organization, even one as well organized with an exemplary history as the Red Cross.

Professor Paul Light from New York University summarized the problem: "The problems that the Red Cross experienced in getting down there involve a lack of investment in technology, a lack of investment in telecommunications, a very serious lack of investment in volunteer training."[2]

IT risk extends well beyond the day-to-day operations of a nonprofit. IT risk can also greatly impact reputational risk. Accidental release or sabotage of confidential stakeholder information can have serious long-term effects. IT needs to be secure, reliable and include a contingency plan as a backup to disruption of service.

Operational Risk Zones

The nonprofits need to pay enough attention to make sure their operations are aligned and effective. Operations have both internal and external outcomes as both good and bad risk.

Let us consider a food bank where employees need to prepare time-consuming and unnecessary reports about each of their activities. Clients may not be affected from this process in the short term, but obviously it will have some internal consequences. The staff will lose their motivation because of the bureaucracy and become frustrated. Similarly consider the opposite case where there is no control at all. This may be more attractive for the staff; however, it will decrease the quality of services in the long term.

Based on our experience, simple tools are very powerful in management practices. Following this rule, we propose the following model to evaluate different operational risks. The model proposes two dimensions. The first dimension is the domain of the risk, and it can be internal or

---

[2]https://www.pbs.org/newshour/show/american-red-cross-troubles (accessed July 22, 2019).

external. The second dimension is related with the resources affiliated with operational risk and uses two categories: human resources or any other type of resources.

As illustrated in Figure 7.1, operational risk can occur in four main groups. The first zone is the internal human resources-related operational risk zone. Not having enough employees for certain administrative jobs is mainly internal. It may have external consequences in the long term; however, for the sake of simplicity, we may prefer to address it internal. This operational risk zone is numbered as 1 in the model.

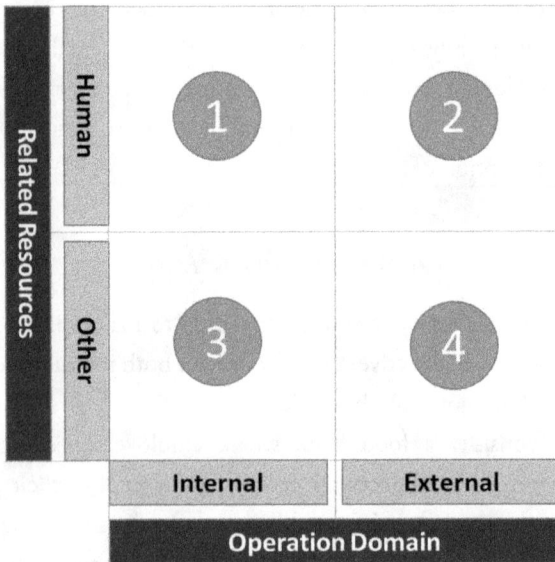

Figure 7.1 Operational risk zones

Similarly, the outdated IT infrastructure may create internal non-human resources-related risks for the nonprofit organizations. The operational risk zone 3 addresses internal operational risks that are caused or related to resources other than human resources.

It is also possible to use the operational risk zones in crossing zones as illustrated in Figure 7.2. For example, not having enough skilled employees in front line is both internal and external risk. Because it affects not only the overall human power needed by the nonprofit organization but also the quality and the quantity of the services provided.

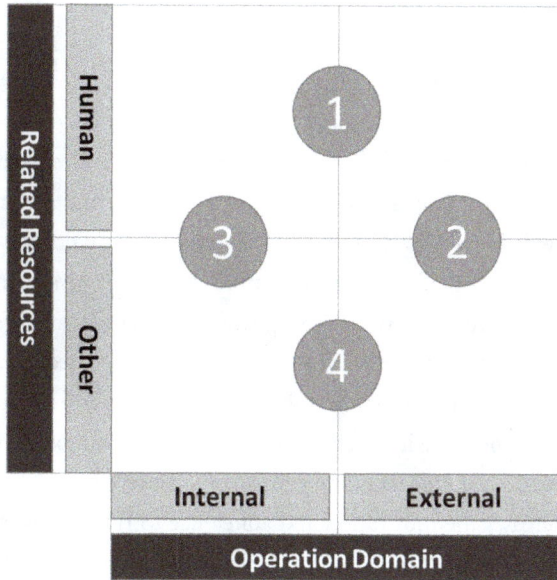

Figure 7.2 Operational risk crossing zones

Of course, other combinations are also possible. We can even talk about certain types of operational risks, which happen in all zones at once. For example, consider the situation illustrated in Figure 7.3.

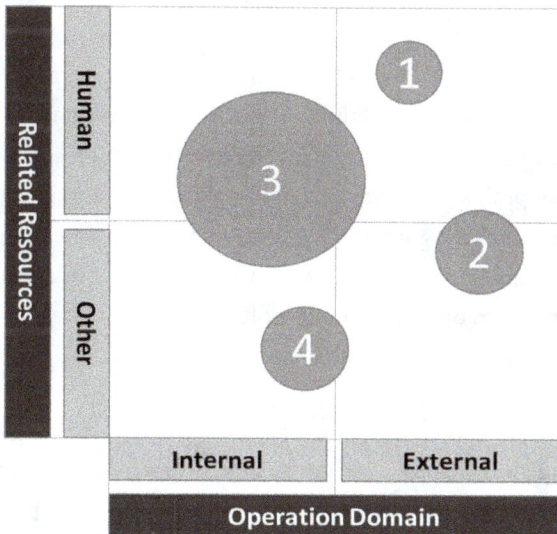

Figure 7.3 Operational risks in all zones

Training

Just as training is essential for the smooth running of operations, so risk training is essential for risk management. Well-trained employees and volunteers are not only efficient but also risk aware. When staff are adequately trained on risk issues, the organization becomes a risk learning one. Staff will be willing to bring risk issues forward and will be more aware of, and more willing to suggest improvements to, risk management procedures. Additionally, risk training can significantly improve the risk culture—an important topic that we discuss in the next section.

The risk component of the training should be composed of two parts: the what to do and the why to do it. The why to do it is almost as important as the what to do. Understanding the "why" creates better risk awareness and also increases the motivation and adherence to risk management procedures. If people understand the consequences of not following procedure, they are more likely to follow it. Additionally, the more they understand about the "why," the better they are able to suggest fruitful improvements.

Specific components of risk training should include discussion of the major risks (both positive risks and negative risks) of the organization, the major risk management activities, as well as a description of the desired risk culture.

Training, particularly when onboarding new staff, is an excellent time to do some of the risk identification and mapping exercises that have been discussed in Chapter 5. Not only does this get the trainees thinking about risk, but it is also an ideal method for getting them to think about of the components of the organization that allow it to function as it does. Even in small nonprofits, there are necessary operational functions that most stakeholders, including internal staff, are almost completely unaware of. Thus, risk training can do double duty: training people about risk and also training them on the full range of functions of the organization.

Risk Culture

We conclude this chapter with a discussion of the risk culture of an organization. The risk culture of an organization is an important part of maintaining a healthy attitude toward risk. While it may seem odd to include culture as part of infrastructure, we have done so as we believe that human capital risk and the risks involved with managing people in a nonprofit are such a critical part of infrastructure. Collectively, the people that constitute a nonprofit, whether they be internal or stakeholders, constitute culture.

Culture encompasses many different aspects. Our concern (although most certainly not the only relevant culture-related concern) is the risk culture. The risk culture is the organization's attitude toward risk. It is the distinction of whether risk is viewed as something to be avoided, the view as to whether all risk is bad, the view as to the consequences of mistakes or accidents, and the view as to the future of the organization. Culture is also whether the organization's people respect risk and are risk aware.

A healthy risk culture is one that respects risk, is risk aware, and understands that risk has a positive as well as a negative aspect to it. A healthy risk culture is willing to try things and to take risks with as much risk intelligence as reasonable. A healthy risk culture does not avoid risk but understands that risks should be managed. A healthy risk culture also understands that some risks need to be managed by process, and other risks need judgment.

An unhealthy risk culture is one that is afraid of risk and is afraid of doing something wrong or incorrectly. An unhealthy risk culture is one that does not want to try things or to develop new methodologies in the hopes of improving outcomes that are in line with the strategic mission. An unhealthy risk culture wants to maintain the status quo despite the fact that it realizes that doing so may be suboptimal.

Culture takes time to develop. It is a combination of the people, the management, and the history of the organization and its culture. Culture is also complex. You cannot mandate culture. The best that you can do is encourage and nurture it.

Discussion of the risk culture, like other components of operational risk, should be an important part of the training and of the onboarding of new staff into the organization.

Concluding Thoughts

Operational risk is the day-to-day management of risk. It is the risk inherent in each of the operational functions of the organization. It may not necessarily be exciting, but it is a critical part of having a risk-healthy firm.

Operational risk is perhaps the broadest part of risk management. It comprises a wide range of functions, types of risk and contains a combination of complicated and complex risks. It requires a judicious mix of process and judgment to successfully manage.

Ultimately, people are at the root of managing operational risk: this is doubly so for a nonprofit, given the servicing component of most of their operations and missions. Unfortunately, the risk culture is an often-neglected yet a critical component of having a positive and productive organization.

CHAPTER 8

Legal, Compliance, and Reputational Risks

Legal, compliance, and reputational risks are critically important to manage for any organization to manage and especially for a nonprofit. While legal and compliance may often be considered simply mandatory, reputational issues can often be what makes or breaks a nonprofit. A nonprofit relies on its reputation to build its relationships with virtually all of its major stakeholders. Volunteers and benefactors in particular will flee if reputation of the nonprofit is not stellar.

Managing legal and reputational risk is ultimately about common sense. Unfortunately, as the saying goes, common sense is not always so common. Particularly in the context of an ever increasingly legalistic society, coupled with the ubiquitous nature of social media, legal, compliance, and reputational risks are ever present, and often in a nuanced form. Furthermore, what may be legally sound may not be reputationally sound and vice versa. Ethical dilemmas can arise where it seems like the nonprofit has no way to universally look good. This is where an explicit emphasis on legal and reputational risk planning can play an important and valuable role in keeping the organization away from such dilemmas.

We begin this chapter with compliance and legal risk, and then build to discuss ideas for managing the more complex reputational risk.

Legal and Compliance Risk

Of the many risks that we discuss in this book, legal and compliance are the least complex in the sense of being a complex system as was discussed in Chapter 1. (Conversely, reputational risk is generally considered to be the most complex of risks.) That does not mean that dealing with legal and compliance risk is easy or straightforward; it simply means that most legal and compliance risk issues can be, and should be, dealt with by experts or specialists. In fact, a whole new industry of RegTech has arisen as entrepreneurial companies are forming to automate the tedious, but complicated tasks of compliance management and also parts of legal management.

The fact that much of legal and compliance can be outsourced to either technology or to experts is a two-edged sword for most nonprofits. To begin with, the resources required for outsourcing may not be available. Additionally, internal expertise may also not be available. If the resources are not available, and must be done internally by nonspecialists, then the legal and compliance function can detract significant time and energy away from the mission of the organization. This is turn leads to staff and volunteer burnout as well as stress.

A second component to legal and compliance risk is that almost everyone appreciates the importance of it. It is also commonly appreciated that legal and compliance has many nuances that are intimidating to most nonexperts in the field. The knowledge that legal and compliance is important, combined with the knowledge that few have the expertise to comprehend it, adds a special feeling of helplessness, which is its own source of stress.

Like most risks, legal and regulatory risk will have different degrees of importance and evoke different levels of comfort with nonprofit managers and directors. Figure 8.1 illustrates a model for thinking about the two main measures of importance and comfort.

The x-axis indicates the level of comfort that the organization has with the legal risk. That comfort could be based on the fact that they either have the personnel who believe that they understand the risk and understand how to manage it, or it could be that the organization believes that the risk is minor or of little significance. The y-axis is for the perceived level of intricacy and the levels of nuance of the risk. This creates four broad zones into which the legal risk can be classified.

Comfort Zone legal risk has low levels of intricacy and the organization is comfortable with the level of risk and their capacity and ability to deal with it. Danger Zone risk, by contrast, has high perceived level of risk, and the level of discomfort to dealing with the risk is high.

Level of intricacy

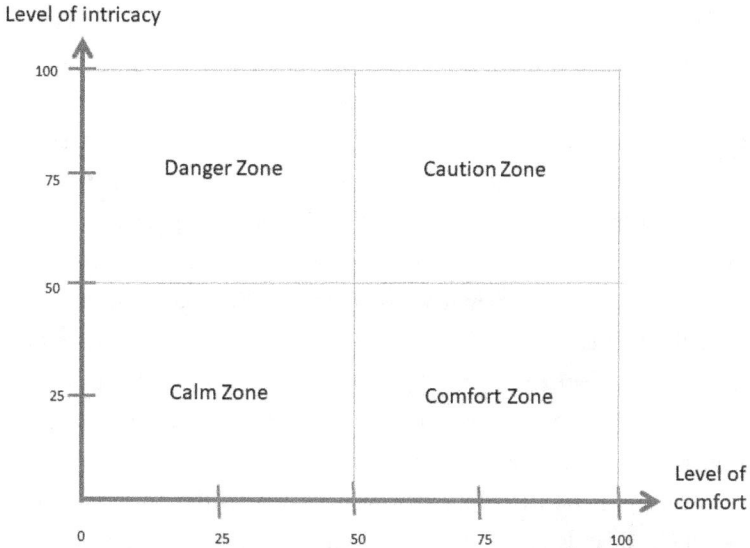

Figure 8.1 Legal comfort and intricacy

The Complacency Zone is where the comfort level is low, but also the perceived legal intricacy is also low. Note that there is an inherent inconsistency in that if you are not comfortable with the legal risk, or equivalently not comfortable with your level of legal understanding, then you likely are not in a position to accurately assess the level of legal intricacy. Finally, there is the Caution Zone. Here the level of legal intricacy is perceived to be high although the level of comfort with the legal risk is also high.

For three of the four zones in Figure 8.1, there is a cause for concern surrounding the legal risk. For these reasons, legal risk is often outsourced. This outsourcing will often be costly, but not outsourcing important legal risks can be even more costly. One issue to ensure that the organization is getting good value is that there should be an assigned contact with the legal provider whose task is to ensure that the appropriate questions are asked, and more importantly that the important legal issues are properly conveyed to the board and to the relevant managers. Just because a legal issue has been outsourced does not mean that it is still not an issue. Legal issues tend to be fluid and nuanced. Frequently, legal solutions imply compromises. These nuances and comprises need to be understood internally as well as externally with the affected stakeholders.

Appointing a board member or a senior manager to regularly report on legal issues is a sound practice for a nonprofit to have. Legal issues, like many risks, tend to only become known when they have become allowed to fester so long that they become a problem. Good risk management, however, is proactive, implementing management techniques before issues become problems and acting to take advantage of opportunities. Furthermore, few managers or board members will get excited about legal issues; this means that they tend to be willfully ignored. Having an appointed member (or team) as well as regularly scheduled updates for a legal and compliance review will prevent these issues from being perpetually pushed to the backburner and will allow the issues to be managed in a much more effective and proactive manner.

A further reason to appoint someone to keep track of legal risk is that the legal landscape is constantly changing, and particularly for those nonprofits that are subject to significant regulation. Given the specialized nature of legal and compliance risk, it is not reasonable to expect a typical staffer to be aware of changes or the implications of those changes.

An aspect of legal risk that is frequently overlooked is that legal risk also has a positive side to it. Large corporations are very active in lobbying and working to change legal and compliance issues, and nonprofits can also play a role in doing so. In fact, given their nature, nonprofits are often granted special access to voice their views. This is a positive risk opportunity for nonprofits that should not be forfeited. Nonprofits can and should be influencers when it comes to legal and compliance change.

Directors' Legal Risk

A direct consequence of the rise of legal and compliance risk issues is an increase in the perceived legal risk of directors. In large part due to the perceived "sleeping on the job" of corporate directors during the corporate debacles of the 1990s, there has been a spin-off effect to the directors of nonprofit organizations. This has significantly changed the risk picture for nonprofits and in many cases made it significantly more difficult to recruit quality directors.

Directors of organizations tend to be almost invisible unless and until something negative happens. Being a director thus has one-way negative risk associated with it. While it is very true that being a director of a nonprofit brings a feeling of goodwill, and of doing one's duty to contribute to society, it is easy to have this goodwill negated by the thought of being potentially caught in a legal or reputational mess. The last thing that someone wants is to volunteer for an organization in the hopes of helping society, but as a result face a costly and painful lawsuit.

Directors' legal risk is complicated by the fact that many directors may not have the expertise to even realize the level of legal risk, or that they even have personal legal risk. Relatedly, prospective board members, while ethical themselves, may be unaware of the ethical and reputational risks of their seemingly innocent actions. As a consequence, well managed nonprofits have legal as well as ethical and reputational risk training as part of the onboarding process for their directors and officers.

The Volunteer Protection Act (VPA) is designed to protect volunteer board members from legal issues when something goes wrong with the nonprofit organization. The purpose of protective regulations is to encourage volunteers to become involved but unfortunately existing laws and regulations do not remove the legal responsibilities of board members, nor can it make them immune from legal issues. Consider the case in 2013 of the Roxbury Comprehensive Community Clinic. This clinic was a nonprofit providing access to health services in the Boston area. Unfortunately it had to close due to financial difficulties. With limited remaining financial resources, the board members decided to use the remaining funds for payments to vendors instead of the employees. As a consequence, the employees filed a suit against board members.[1]

The primary piece of directors' legal risk management is now a standard directors and officers insurance policy. While policies vary extensively, "D&O" policies as they are commonly known, provide a level of protection and it is something that most credible directors will insist on having before joining a nonprofit board.

D&O insurance in its most basic form covers directors against the costs and damages of a lawsuit. What D&O insurance does not, and indeed cannot cover, is the reputational risk that a director may take in

---

[1]https://nonprofitquarterly.org/board-member-and-volunteer-liability-the-case-of-roxcomp/ (accessed July 17, 2019).

the court of public perception if the organization is sued; even if the suit is found to be baseless, frivolous or without merit.

A side effect of having D&O insurance is that it brings risk management, both of the personal variety, as well as the risk management of the nonprofit, to the attention of both new and experienced directors. Many nonprofit directors are serving because they believe in the mission or service of the nonprofit, and not based on any special experience or expertise that they may have. In fact, many directors of nonprofits may have very limited directorship or even managerial experience and may be naively unaware of the larger aspect of risks they and the organization may have to deal with. Having to sign a D&O insurance policy frequently brings the risks into focus in an emphatic manner.

Ethics

Another fallout from the corporate debacles of the 1990s, and emphasized by ongoing issues since, is that of ethics. Ethics risk has become a key risk, and such an important subset of reputational risk, that it deserves mention as a separate category.

Ethics is one-part awareness and one-part character. Many claim that the ethical breaches in business were the fault of academic and professional schools not teaching ethics. This may have played a small role, but there is more to ethics than just training. For instance, Bernie Madoff, a fund manager who operated a Ponzi scheme that imploded in 2008, is often put forward as the poster boy for someone who needed to be taught ethics for his violation of financial trading rules and proper bookkeeping. However, Bernie Madoff was in charge of the rules committee at the exchange where he conducted his trades; he knew the rules as well, or better, than anyone! The Madoff example clearly shows that training does not solve the problem of an ethically challenged character. Managing ethical risk has two components; training for awareness and consistency, and ensuring staff has the proper ethical character to begin with.

What passes for proper ethics (as well as proper etiquette) changes as the context of the times change. A simple example is the ethics of smoking in public places. Thirty years ago, it was common practice to smoke just about any place. Now of course it is completely unacceptable, and indeed illegal in many cities, to smoke in public places and even public spaces outdoors. Thus, ethical guidelines need to be frequently updated and modified to ensure that they are consistent with current standards.

For global organizations ethics may involve regional nuances and customs that need to be accounted for. While it is desirable to have global standards of practice, it can be difficult at times to put into universal practice depending on the scope of the organization. There have been several well-publicized cases of bribes, which are well accepted in many parts of the world, being a source of embarrassment to both for-profit as well as nonprofit organizations.

Having ethical training available for staff and directors, or an organizational ethics handbook is a key risk management tool. As with most risk management procedures, the board should approve and occasionally review the ethics guidelines and principles of the organization. Depending on the scope of the organization's activities, many ethical guidelines templates are readily and freely available and could be used with little or no modifications.

As with other risk management tools, the idea is not to overburden the organization with procedures that are unduly harsh or constraining. It is difficult, however, to overstress the importance of ethics. Fortunately, good ethics can be clearly spelled out simply and should be the default operating principles of people in general.

Special ethical situations that may arise out of the specific operations of the organization should be particularly emphasized. These would include things such as situations that volunteers may have limited experience with. Examples could be dealing with the religious customs of immigrants or the handling of people with physical or intellectual impairments.

One special ethical case involves former Vice President Joe Biden. Before he began his 2019 quest to be the Democratic nominee for the 2020 Presidential campaign, Mr. Biden and his wife dropped their association with the Biden Cancer Institute, a nonprofit set up to create partnerships between government, industry and academic stakeholders in order to find cures for cancer. It was believed that maintaining a relationship with the nonprofit that he helped to set up would comprise a breach of ethics for a Presidential campaigner. However, without the direct support of the Bidens, the support for the initiative quickly waned. This made continuing with its mission impossible and it was quickly decided to cease operations.[2]

The current social context requires a special mention of respectful workplace environment policies. The #MeToo and #BlackLivesMatter movements, among many other of their kind, have brought again to the fore the importance of respectful and inclusive workplaces. Needless to say, this extends to nonprofit organizations. Diversity, inclusion, and respectfulness has rightly become an important issue for many organizations.

In certain cases, diversity issues can lead to ethical dilemmas. A well-publicized example is that of the Boy Scouts and their removal of the ban on openly gay Scout leaders.[3] Traditionally a church-based organization, with Scout meetings commonly held in church halls and significant level of support from those churches, the issue of openly gay leaders was a divisive issue with passionately held views on both sides. Some of the affiliated churches were for the ban, while other affiliated churches were passionately against the ban. The fact that the beneficiaries of the organization are young boys of an impressionable age was obviously an important consideration. There are also legal issues surrounding discrimination to consider. This was a true ethical dilemma for the organization and one that will likely continue to be an ongoing issue for some time.

True ethical dilemmas are almost a special case of ethics. Fortunately, they tend to be rare, but when they do occur, their effect can be very divisive and devastating. There are various frameworks for dealing with ethical dilemmas, but the situations tend to be very idiosyncratic that a general framework is generally of limited help. True ethical dilemmas are generally a case for the whole board to wrestle with along with the help of managers and relevant staff.

The reality is that people vary in their ethics due to their experience or their backgrounds. This brings up the staffing component of ensuring good ethics. This has three parts: ensuring that there is reasonable level of background checks before onboarding, training as appropriate, and having a policy in place to offboard those who show lapses in ethical behavior.

[2]https://apnews.com/97adeafe979943808a3abe963e089135 (accessed July 17, 2019).
[3]https://www.theglobeandmail.com/news/world/us-boy-scouts-committee-ends-ban-on-gay-leaders-larger-board-must-ratify-change/article25497614/ (accessed July 17, 2019).

The extent of background checks depends on the level of the risk. Generally, a recommendation from someone within the organization will be sufficient. However, in special cases, such as when staff or volunteers will be left with minors, then additional background checks should be made. It should be a defined policy of the organization what level of background checks are appropriate. High quality potential volunteers and staffers have come to expect such checks. If they have issues with background checks, then it is likely best that they do not work for the organization. Having said that, it is important to reiterate that the level of the background check is in line with the nature of the tasks to be done by the potential volunteer or staffer. An extensive and intrusive background check for a volunteer who is to be tasked with maintenance of a community soccer field would likely send any volunteer looking for another organization to help. An organization where adult volunteers will be left alone with children is the type of organization where it is reasonable to expect volunteers to undergo a background check. For instance, Scouts Canada has a relatively extensive volunteer screening program that it requires of all volunteers who will be in a position of trust within its organization.[4]

Ethics training is the second leg of a healthy and ethical organization. In the for-profit sector, ethics and diversity training has become mandatory at an increasing number of organizations. Typically, onboarding staff are mandated to complete watching a set of videos and then answer a series of multiple-choice questions that certify that they did indeed watch the videos. It is easy to become cynical of such training. We believe that ethics training should suit the situation and context of the organization. It is our belief that the vast number of people want to be good citizens and want to be ethical in their treatment of others. Additionally, the majority of people have the good common sense to know what constitutes proper ethical behavior in the vast majority of situations. Thus, it is only the specialized training that is context specific that is generally required.

As part of the training, it is also helpful to have a handbook of ethics that each employee and volunteer could be asked to read and sign their agreement to. The ethics handbook could include not only ethical

---

[4]https://www.scouts.ca/resources/support-resources/bpp/policies/volunteer-screening-policy.html (accessed November 20, 2019).

components but also elements of a respectful workplace document as well as a section on reputational risk.

The third part of an ethics risk strategy is to have a process in place to deal with a member of the board, management, or staff that has demonstrated a lapse of ethics. Ethical lapses obviously differ in their severity and could range from an innocent and unintended remark that was misinterpreted to outright and planned egregious behavior. It could also be behavior or events that occurred outside of the organization's activities. For instance, a volunteer of a religious nonprofit could publicly engage in behavior explicitly banned by the religion that the nonprofit is set up to serve.

A risk-focused organization will have a plan as well as decision-making panel in place to deal with significant cases. Responses could range from a gentle aside with the offender to additional training resources, to outright disassociation with the individual. Hopefully, with proper onboarding, and with appropriate training, such instances are rare, but it is much easier to deal with them when they do if a plan is already in place than to manage without a plan in real time.

A final part of ethics risk management is to keep a running log or risk register of ethical issues. Such a log helps build awareness of ethical risks, can serve as future training pieces, and helps the risk management team of the nonprofit develop a picture of the common ethical risks so they can better plan their risk management strategy.

When constructing the ethics policy, one should not forget to include a section on environmental responsibility to the extent that it may be an issue. Good ethics and environmental responsibility are all part of the larger picture of good organizational social responsibility and governance. It is also becoming an important part of reputational risk.

Having a separate respectful environment policy from the ethics document is likely a reasonable idea for most organizations. Again, there are many excellent templates that are readily available. The point is not to add layers of document bureaucracy, but to emphasize that good ethics extends to good manners for all.

Before leaving ethics, it is important to note that effective legal risk management is not necessarily good ethical risk management and vice versa. An organization can be in excellent legal standing, yet still be acting unethically. Likewise, they can be acting perfectly ethically while being afoul of the law. There is a general principle of acting in the spirit of the law versus acting to the letter of the law. This may come out not only in a legal manner but also in a reputational manner. The general public generally does not have the full contextual information, nor do they generally understand the legal and ethical nuances of an issue. This creates the potential for an unintended reputational risk. Ethics, compliance and legal risk comes down to asking not only, "Are we doing the right things?" but additionally, "Are we being perceived as doing the right things?"

Reputational Risk

The rise of social media and the effect it can have on the reputation of an organization is hard to overstate. Organizations of all types use social media for a variety of valuable uses from general getting the message out to recruiting employees and volunteers. Social media can almost instantly give even the smallest of organizations global exposure. This makes social media a very powerful tool. It also makes social media a very dangerous weapon that can backfire against even the most cautious of users. Social media is definitely an area of two-sided risk when it comes to setting the reputational risk of the firm.

When it comes to social media risk's relationship to reputational risk, training can be a valuable tool. Many people, unless they are public figures, do not have an appreciation for how quickly reputational risks can spiral out of control due to what may be considered an otherwise benign social media post. (Of course, many public figures are not immune from inappropriate social media activity.) Making people simply aware of the potential consequences of social media and reputational risk is generally sufficient. As an added layer of risk management, the organization may wish to develop a set of social media guidelines.

Reputational risk of course extends well beyond social media activity. Again, simple training is often all that is needed. The age-old maxim of acting as if all of your actions will be reported on the front page of the newspaper (and updated to include an assumption that all of your actions will become a trending meme on social media) is often the only basis of training that is needed.

Changes in reputational risk often come as a total surprise. Reputational risk is not something that gets mentioned in many risk reports, but for nonprofits it is critical. One way to ensure that reputational risk is on everyone's radar is to make it an explicit part of any risk mapping exercise.

Reputational risk is almost always complex in nature. As such it is a risk that cannot be solved but instead must be constantly managed. There are no easy steps to take to reduce reputational risk beyond awareness and common sense. As it can change in an instant, it is prudent to have a reputational crisis management team ready to respond if a reputational risk does present itself. Being unprepared to deal with a reputational risk will generally negatively compound the problems. There should be a clear chain of command as to who is to manage reputational risk in the case of a crisis and how they are going to manage it. As the old saying goes, it takes lifetime to build a reputation but only a minute to destroy it.

Concluding Thoughts

Legal, compliance, and reputational risks may not be the "fun" parts of risk management, but that does not make them less important. While legal and compliance risks are "complicated," in the sense that they follow known rules and laws, the equally important reputational risks are complex in that they exhibit evidence of emergence and there are no rules or laws for ensuring good reputational management.

Legal, compliance, and reputational risks are based on awareness. Many well-intentioned volunteers and staffers are simply out of their normal context while acting on behalf of the nonprofit organization. Making sure everyone is aware of potential issues goes a long way toward effective management of these risks.

CHAPTER 9

Risk Treatment

The evidence seemed to be quite clear. The injury statistics coming from the sport of rugby seemed obvious to the members of the Nova Scotia (Canada) school board. Rugby-related injury rates were far higher than for hockey or even than those for football. Especially troubling were the rates for concussions. The concern was not only for the health and safety of student athletes but also that insurance rates would soar and put the entire sports activities of all students in jeopardy. There was only one thing that seemed reasonable to do, and that was to immediately shut down rugby as an official school sport. An announcement was drawn up, and even though it was just weeks until the end of the rugby season and the provincial championships, the declaration was made that all rugby games were suspended, and the sport would no longer be a sanctioned school sport.[1] The decision was presented as being final.

The situation facing the Nova Scotia school board required a decision as to how to respond to a perceived risk. The possible range of responses to risk is quite broad, and as we shall subsequently discuss for the Nova Scotia school board, the responses to this particular risk of rugby injuries run the full gamut from eliminate to embrace. As we will see, the decisions facing the Nova Scotia school board in terms of what to do about the sport of high school rugby provide an interesting case study in the decisions around risk treatment.

In this chapter we cover the main responses to risk. In many books on risk management, the responses range from ignore to eliminate. With our belief that the focus on risk should be both positive and negative, the possible range of appropriate responses is much greater. The various

---

[1]https://www.thechronicleherald.ca/news/local/nova-scotia-high-school-rugby-brought-to-a-halt-mid-season-insurance-concerns-cited-307984/ (accessed July 21, 2019).

treatments of risk, from avoidance to mitigation, risk enhancement, and even embracing risk, are discussed in this chapter. A key focus of this chapter (and indeed throughout the book) is ensuring that the risk management elements are aligned with the strategic objectives of the organization.

Deciding the appropriate response to a risk, and the intensity of the response is a key part of effective risk management. As discussed in Chapter 5, not all risks should be treated equally, nor should they be given the same amount of attention or resources. Some risks have the potential for large impact, while others will have minimal to no impact. Some risks directly affect the achievement of objectives, while other risks may be significant, but not to the specific objectives of the organization. For some risks there simply may be little to nothing that can be done except acknowledging and accepting them, and putting in place appropriate contingency or response plans for when they come to fruition.

Choosing a level of response to a given risk seems like a straightforward or perhaps even trivial task. However, deciding on a risk response not only sets the managerial tactics involved in managing that specific risk but also plays a role in setting the risk culture for the organization. If it is made clear that the organization actively considers a range of responses for different types of risk, then risks will more clearly and transparently come to the fore for risk management consideration. Having an expanded range of risk responses shows that the organization has an objective and open-minded attitude toward risk and, in turn, this makes risk management discussions more productive and fruitful. Having a range of responses also increases the creativity in which the board, the management, the staff, and the stakeholders of the organization are compelled to think about risk, which, in turn, leads to more thoughtful and effective risk management.

Risk treatment is composed of three phases as illustrated in Figure 9.1. The detection phase includes the identification and grouping of the risk. It also determines whether the detected risk is over predetermined thresholds or not as explained in detail further in this chapter.

The second phase of the risk treatment is the decision of how to respond to the risk and is the main focus of this chapter. This chapter will explore some methodologies to make this process less subjective and more effective. Finally, the last step of the risk treatment is the action where the risk response decision is implemented.

Figure 9.1 Risk treatment phases

Strategic Evaluation of Risk

Not being able to see the woods for the trees is a common management disorder. Nonprofits are not exempt from this disease. Giving a lot of attention to trees and being away from the fullness of the forest is an inevitable result of spending all resources for operational management and having no time for strategic management.

Regarding risk, a strategic approach can be used in two ways: managing strategic risk and managing risk strategically. The former one focuses only on the risk that has strategic consequences and ignores the operational level risks whereas the latter one approaches both operational and strategic risk with a unified strategic perspective. In this book we promote the methodology of managing risk strategically.

Consider the case of the board of education and their decision of how to respond to injuries in high school rugby. Strategically, one assumes that one of their main strategies is the healthy development of all school-age children. At an operational level there was an apparent risk in the level of rugby injuries, but there were also the beneficial risks of the physical, emotional, and leadership development that was experienced by rugby participants. It is a clear case where there are benefits from managing risk strategically.

Similar to other management practices, risk management also requires optimization of resources. One way of using resources effectively is ensuring the alignment between risks and strategies. The following simple matrix in Table 9.1 can be utilized to determine how an organization's risks and strategies are related.

In our example we can see that Risk A is related only with Strategy C, and Risk C is related only with Strategy B. Risks can be related to

Table 9.1 Risks versus strategies matrix

	Strategy A	Strategy B	Strategy C	Strategy D
Risk A			X	
Risk B	X		X	
Risk C		X		
Risk D				

multiple strategies as well. Risk B, for example is both related with Strategy A and Strategy C.

The same matrix is also useful to determine when there is no connection between a risk and any of the strategies. In this case we can address it as a misalignment between risk management and strategic management. All risks should be related at least to one of the strategies. If a risk is not related with any of the strategies it is probably because of wrong risk identification and/or wrong strategic planning. For instance, in the matrix in Table 9.1, Risk D is not aligned with any of the organization's strategies, and thus there is a need to question why the organization is continuing the activity that is giving rise to the risk.

Finally, the same matrix can also be used to compare the total risk of each strategy. In the example, Strategy D has no risks associated meaning that Strategy D can be implemented without any significant risk. On the other hand, both Risk A and Risk B are related to Strategy C as the riskiest strategy based on the assumption that all risks are identical in terms of impact, probability, and level of control. This approach can be an additional tool for decision makers when they try to prioritize strategies. A Risk versus Strategies matrix is a simple but efficient tool to match risks with strategies and illustrate synergies and efficiencies.

Risk Tolerance and Risk Appetite

Two important concepts are generally part of any discussion of risk treatment: risk tolerance and risk appetite. Various authors and risk consultants use these terms in varying ways, so it is important to make clear at the outset what we mean by each of the terms.

Risk tolerance refers to those risks that the organization will not tolerate under any circumstances. Dramatic examples may include a risk that could cause harm to the health of a stakeholder. As another example it could be something that causes a risk such that a religious tenet will be broken or be counter to a fundamental belief of the organization. In any case, there will be certain risks that an organization will be exposed to that it will determine that it simply will not tolerate if at all possible. In our case study of high school rugby, the risk tolerance could be drawn at serious and permanent injury of a student athlete.

When discussing risk tolerance, it is important to note that accidents and mishaps will happen no matter what, and the only way that an organization can be completely free from all risk is to cease operations (which bring into play a host of other risks related to not appropriately serving the intended beneficiaries). Some organizations attempt to thus quantify the probability around a risk tolerance. For instance, many organizations will put a one-hundredth of a percent probability of an event based on their risk tolerance happening. For instance, if the risk tolerance was set at one-hundredth percent of a death occurring, this would mean statistically that one out of every 10,000 times that there would be a death. This is about three times *less* likely than the odds of someone being struck by lightning in their lifetime. We expand on this concept later in the chapter when we discuss risk threshold.

When we get to these very low probabilities, then we are in the range of what are known as tail events. Tail events are very rare events that may or may not have a large impact. Tail events that have a large impact are known as black swans.[2] A prime example of a black swan is the events of September 11, 2001 when the planes commandeered by terrorists flew into the World Trade Center. This was a low probability event that had a very large impact. A happier black swan event would be the example of someone winning the lottery; again, a very low probability event that will have a huge impact on the rest of their life.

It is very difficult to estimate the probabilities of tail events. They happen so rarely, and furthermore they tend to be very idiosyncratic. These characteristics mean that it is usually not possible to detect patterns from which reliable models, statistics, or even estimates of probability

---

[2] N. Taleb. 2010. *The Black Swan: The Impact of the Highly Improbable* (New York, NY: Random House Inc.).

of occurring can be made. The point is not to get too caught up in the mathematics or the logistics of managing tail events, and to realize that it is simply not possible to eliminate all risks by any reasonable means. However, the list of risks that violate the organization's risk tolerance list should as far as practical be considered verboten.

The second concept is that of risk appetite. Risk appetite is the amount of overall risk that the organization is willing to accept as they go about their daily operations. There is no correct or optimum level for risk appetite. Some organizations will be comfortable with a lot of risk, and some will be comfortable with only small levels of risk. Like individuals, each organization will have a specific level of risk that they feel comfortable with.

It is generally relatively easy for an organization to come up with a list of risks that they will not tolerate. These will be based upon generally acceptable risks that are widely considered unacceptable. Conversely, determining the risk appetite is generally a completely subjective matter. First, it is subjective as there is no overall objective measure of risk for the organization as a whole. Second, there is no objective way to state what the optimal level should be even if such an objective risk measure existed.

When determining the risk appetite, the board, with advice from management and other stakeholders, has to go more by intuition than by an objective and rational analysis. Factors that would advocate for a greater risk appetite, all else being equal, is stability and security in funding, experience of the organization and the experience of its management team and staff, as well as the nature of its activities, with lower in risk nature activities arguing for a more aggressive risk appetite than might otherwise be the case. The more uncertain and stable the sources of funding, the more the inexperience in the organization and riskier activities in general for the organization, indicating that a smaller risk appetite may be more appropriate. The irony, of course, is that reality and circumstances often force the underfunded and immature nonprofit organization to have a larger risk appetite than they would like in order to allow the organization to grow and develop a foothold in its activities and to achieve its mission.

The risk tolerance and the risk appetite are functions for the board to not only set but also have managerial oversite over. Both the risk tolerance and the risk appetite are strategic decisions. They concern the culture of the organization as well as the long-term direction of the organization. They also set the tone for the rest of risk management.

Revisiting the Risk Map

The risk map for the organization is the starting point for developing risk responses. The risk map was discussed in Chapter 5. The risk map shows the impact, the probability, as well as the conceptual amount of control that the organization has for each of its risks.

Every organization likely has more risks than it can handle at one time. Thus, there is a need for the prioritization of the risks and prioritization for the risk management plan. The risk map provides a visual guide to begin the analysis.

A common technique to spot the types of risks is a heat map. A heat map, illustrated in Figure 9.2, plots the negative risks as in a risk map, but with the negative risks only. The impact is still on the horizontal axis, but now values farther to the right are considered to be riskier. The plot of the risks are then separated into green, yellow, and red zones. Risks in Figure 9.1 that have a high probability of occurring and a large negative impact (and replotted on the heat map) are considered to be Red Zone risks that need to be prioritized in their management. Conversely, risks that have a low negative impact as well as a low probability of occurring are considered to be Green Zone risks that can be given

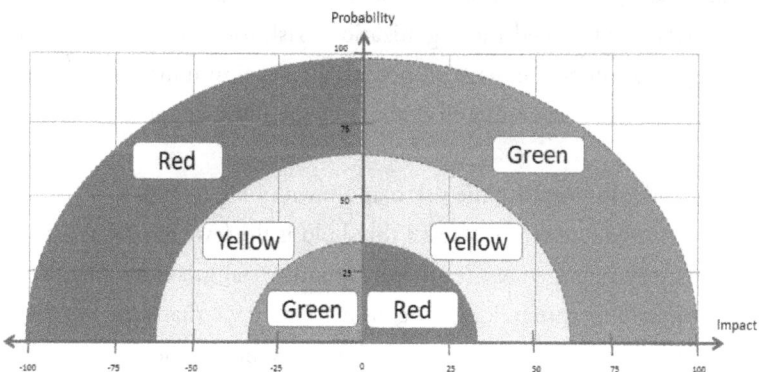

Figure 9.2 Heat map

lower priority or perhaps even ignored. Risks that have medium negative impact and medium probability of occurring are Yellow Zone risks. These are risks that should be managed but have lower priority than Red Zone risks.

Consider now risks in the area of positive risk with a small probability of occurring and a small impact. What if those risks could be managed to increase their probability as well as its impact? For instance, think of the risk of the self-esteem that young adults can get from playing rugby. Unlike many sports where a certain body type is required, the sport of rugby is unique in that the variety of positions on a team mean that almost any body type can play and be successful. This is especially true for females that play rugby. The positive physical fitness outcomes, as well as the self-esteem and character building that team sports develops in high schoolers can be immense. This is a risk that should be enhanced and built upon by encouraging more schools to support the sport and to increase the number of teams and thus players involved in the sport. An organization should ask if it is possible to manage its positive risks so that they move on the risk map to a position with greater probability and greater impact. If so, then this is a risk that should be prioritized for risk management due to the strong positive impact it can have.

Risk Threshold

Taking the previous discussion of risk maps further is the concept of risk thresholds. As discussed earlier, it is not practical, nor is it feasible to completely eliminate risk without some associated costs; even those risks that exceed the organization's risk tolerance. Additionally, no organization can manage all potential risks simultaneously because of their limited resources and because of the impracticality of such an approach.

Consider for instance the risk map shown in Figure 9.3.

The dotted line can be set as a threshold is the level of probability. In certain cases, management teams may ignore certain risks that are below some probability threshold. Now consider Figure 9.4 that shows a similar concept for the impact of the risks. It illustrates the thresholds for positive

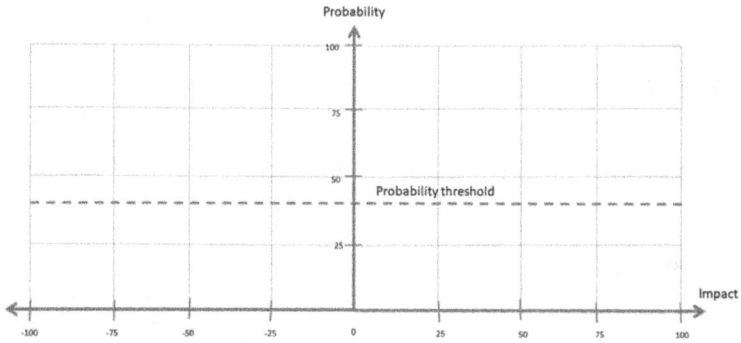

Figure 9.3 Probability thresholds

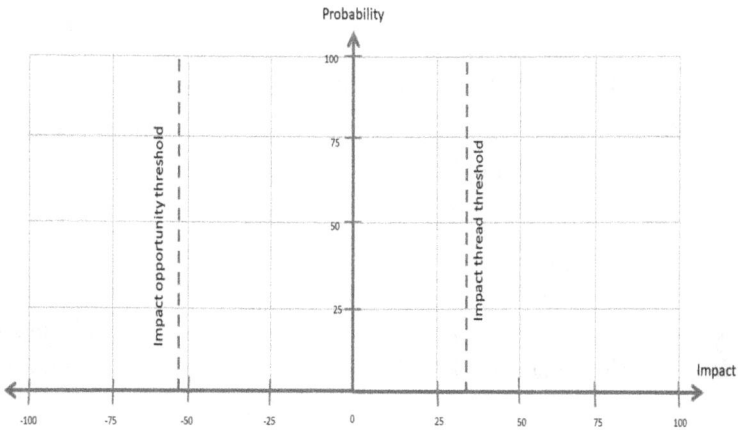

Figure 9.4 Impact thresholds

and negative risk (opportunity). It is natural to have a threshold on positive side too because risk with low positive impact may not seem attractive to decision makers unless there is a way to shift upward the level of positive impact.

Another factor that needs to be recognized in our example is that the threshold on positive and negative sides are not identical. The risk perception and thresholds may be different for positive and negative risk.

In real life, decisions are generally based not only on probability or impact but both. It is also based on the ability to control, affect or otherwise manage the risk.

Allocating Resources

One of the major steps of risk treatment is the allocation of resources. A table similar to that shown in Table 9.2 will be useful for the initial identification of needed resources. Once the simple table is ready the nonprofit organization can proceed with the detailed steps.

Table 9.2 *Risks versus resources matrix*

	Funding	Staff	Volunteers	Marketing	Time	Focus
Risk A						
Risk B						
Risk C						
Risk D						

This methodology will help nonprofit organizations to prioritize their risk treatment activities, which is different than risk prioritization. Risk analysis is the first level of our risk management framework, which includes the determination of risks to be managed. The prioritization of the risks at this initial phase will be based on the analysis.

Risk priorities need to be reexamined frequently as the nature of risks are dynamic and constantly changing. For example, a nonprofit organization with enough number of staff may consider lacking volunteers as a low priority risk. However, a temporary load on the operations and unexpected departure of staff members may increase the need for immediate volunteers. In this case the priority of the risk of not having enough volunteers will increase. Due to dynamic changes in the conditions nonprofit managers need to be ready to adjust their risk priorities.

The BEST Model

Risk treatment can be done in many ways based on the available resources and conditions. When there are more than one alternative to response to an occurring risk, nonprofit management teams may experience difficulty in prioritizing alternatives. One of the models that can be used is called BEST, which is composed of the initials of the four parameters that are used for the evaluation: Benefits, Efforts, Strategic Importance, and Time.

The BEST model is a quantitative tool to make prioritization process less subjective and more manageable. As illustrated in the Figure 9.5, it allows all alternatives to plot on one single graph and make comparisons. In contrast to one dimensional prioritization tools, the BEST model doesn't use lists but rather a graph that is used as a decision support system. It aids decision makers of a nonprofit organization in deciding which alternatives will be implemented and which alternatives will be eliminated.

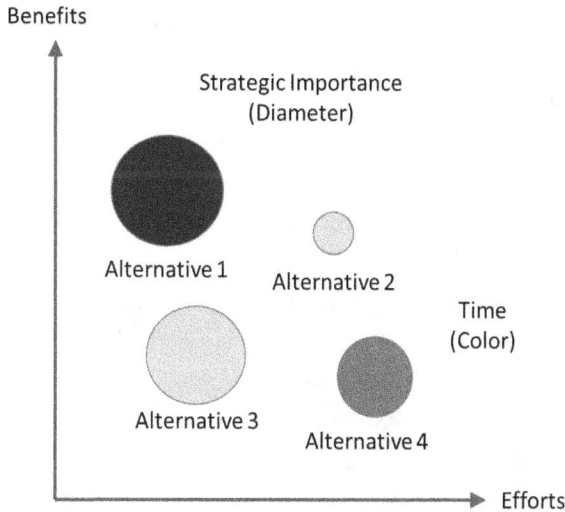

Figure 9.5 Risk versus resources matrix

The two axes of the graph illustrate the level of benefit and effort required to implement a particular alternative. In the example there are four alternatives where Alternative 1 has the highest benefit and in return the lowest effort. Alternative 4 on the other hand requires the highest effort but has low benefits in return.

The third dimension is the strategic importance and indicated with the size of the circle. The bigger the size of the circle, the more strategically important the alternative is for the nonprofit organization. According to the example, Alternative 1 has high strategic importance for the nonprofit organization, whereas Alternative 2 has the lowest.

Let's consider an example to have a better understanding about what strategic importance really means. Imagine a case where a charity that offers jobs to people with disabilities experiences difficulties in finding new staff who has any kind of disability. One alternative may be hiring people who are not disabled. This may solve the problem but obviously will not match with the strategic objectives of the charity. The board and the managers may still prefer this alternative if this is better than the other alternatives; however, they will be aware of the shift from their original objectives.

Finally the fourth dimension is time. Sometimes nonprofit organizations have time limitations, which prevents them from selecting the best option if time was not an issue. The darkness of the filled color indicates how long it will take for each alternative. In the example Alternative 1 is the darkest, which means will take longer than the other two. Color coding may vary for each organization but just as an example let's say dark blue indicates more than 1 year, blue indicates 6 months to 1 year and light blue indicates 6 months or less.

If time was not an issue, the best option on the example would be Alternative 1, which has the highest benefits and strategic importance whereas the efforts needed is the lowest. If the decision makers of the organization need a quicker action then they may select one of the other alternatives depending on their decision-making criteria.

As can be seen, the BEST model functions as a decision support system but not necessarily as a decision system. This implies that nonprofit managers need to be aware about the conditions and objectively compare alternatives and still have the authority to make the final decision.

Return on Risk Investment

A return on risk investment measure is another aid for decision making about risk and what risks to prioritize. A return on risk measure provides one method to rank risks in terms of their priority in terms of improving risk management in relation to the resources spent on risk management.

To calculate a return on risk investment, simply divide the change in risk score, divided by the resources attached to change the risk score as shown in Figure 9.6.[3]

---

[3] A similar concept called "Risk Bang for the Buck" as applied at the public utility Hydro One is outlined in T. Aabo, J.R.S. Fraser, and B.J. Simkins. 2005. "The Rise and Evolution of the Chief Risk Officer: Enterprise Risk Management at Hydro One." *Journal of Applied Corporate Finance* 17, no. 3, pp. 62-75.

$$\text{Return on risk investment} = \frac{\text{Change in risk score}}{\text{Investment in risk resources used on risk}}$$

Figure 9.6 Return on risk investment equation

The risk score has been previously discussed in Chapter 5, "Risk Analytics." The change in risk score is how much the risk score is estimated to change after a risk management strategy has been applied to it. The denominator of the equation in Figure 9.6 is the resources, including both monetary resources as well as time and material resources, which are necessary to implement the proposed risk strategy. Note that there may be several different proposed risk strategies to manage the risk, all of which may require different amount of resources and change the risk score by differing amounts.

The return on risk investment is a useful method to rank alternative strategies for managing risk and to guide the organization in where they should spend their time, resources, and energies on risk management. Not every risk can be, or should be, a priority for risk management. As the old saying goes, if everything is a priority, then nothing is a priority.

Before getting into the specifics of the different ways to treat risk, it is important to note that some risks need to be managed. Those that involve regulatory, legal, moral, or ethical concerns must be managed and should not be part of a prioritization. These risks are mandatory to manage; the only discussion in their management should be the most efficient and effective management method for which the return on risk investment metric may be useful.

Internal Management versus Outsourcing Risk Management

After deciding which risks it needs to prioritize, the next task is to decide whether it is a task that the organization should manage itself or if it should outsource the management of certain risks. This is where a key understanding of the objectives of the organization, the key skills and services that are its reason for existence, and the objectives of the risk management function all come together. It also depends on the nature of the risk, the expertise and resources it takes to effectively manage, the existing level of internal expertise among the staff, and the relative return from managing the risk internally versus outsourcing the risk.

Outsourcing a risk means to let an external organization take care of either the function that is causing the risk or to outsource the management of the risk itself. For instance, the risk of ticket sales for a performing arts group may be outsourced to a promotional company that has the resources and the marketing expertise to more effectively manage the ticket sales and create a higher probability of sufficient ticket sales. Likewise, purchasing insurance to cover the costs of accidents would be a common example of outsourcing the risk itself.

Outsourcing a risk generally involves costs. For instance, an event promotion company will charge either a flat fee or a percentage of ticket sales (or both) and insurance premiums will need to be paid for insurance. The decision to outsource risk management will frequently depend on the cost of outsourcing the risk versus the costs of managing the risk inhouse.

There is another major consideration beyond the cost of outsourcing risk, and that is whether or not the management of the risk is a critical skill for the organization to have. In the for-profit world, companies can easily be virtual companies and outsource almost every aspect of their operations. Apple for instance, does not manufacture any of its devices and is basically a concept and design company, with the actual development and manufacture of products and apps being left to external sources that may or may not be directed by Apple managers. It is an attractive business model for many for-profit companies and it is one that many nonprofit organizations are increasingly considering. The key point is to make sure that the critical skills for success are retained within the organization. The same is true for nonprofits and the argument extends to the critical skills of risk management.

Outsourcing is a very seductive alternative for risk management. However, costs and the potential loss of critical skills are arguments against risk outsourcing. This is where a return on risk investment calculation is helpful.

Returning for a moment to the case of the Nova Scotia school board and its rugby issue, the response from students was shock, quickly followed by action. Within 24 hours a social media campaign had begun, and rallies were planned for the following day in front of the provincial legislature. Parents, coaches, and especially players and fellow students made sure that they were not going to accept the decision to suspend and end the rugby season lightly. The nonprofit provincial rugby association (which was unaffiliated with high school rugby or the school board) also got involved. The Provincial Chief Medical Officer also spoke publicly on the issue as well as several trauma physicians.

The message was clear and consistent that the positive risks of rugby far outweighed the negative risks. It appeared that the reported statistics for rugby as compared to other school sports was more a consequence of the rigorous record keeping of the rugby coaches and the underreporting of injuries from the other sports, most notably hockey and football, which were used by comparison to make the judgment to cancel rugby. The fact also came to light that rugby was one of the few sports that was especially popular with female participants.

The Nova Scotia school board now had not only a health and safety risk decision to be made but had also created a reputational risk and potentially a charge of sexism. The board did not look good in how they made the initial decision, or in their command of the facts and stakeholder management. The furor became so loud that the provincial minister of education stepped in, overruled the board of education, and stated that rugby as a high school sport was most certainly to continue.

This is when creative risk thinking and considering a full range of risk responses kicked in. The provincial rugby association was able to control the high school rugby activities for the short remainder of the year and run the provincial tournament. This is a prime example of outsourcing an unwanted risk. The Education Board got rid of a risk that they did not understand and were not comfortable with. The provincial rugby association (at the time of this writing) is running high school rugby and will likely bring about some positive changes, and students not only saw their beloved sport reinstated but also learnt something about positive civic action. We will revisit the case of Nova Scotia high school rugby later in this chapter, as there are still more risk lessons to be learnt from this episode.

Risk Responses

We tend to think in terms of five generic risk responses; eliminate/avoid/reduce, mitigate, ignore, enhance, and leverage/embrace as illustrated in Figure 9.7.

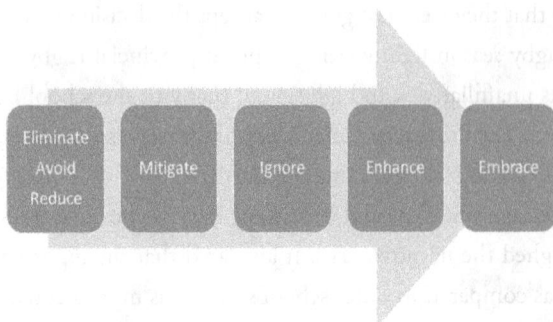

Figure 9.7 Risk responses

Eliminate/Avoid/Reduce

The risks with negative impact you obviously want to reduce in some way. The questions are how many resources are available to expend and how much of a priority it is to reduce the risk. For risks that surpass the risk tolerance, you want to eliminate them to the fullest practical extent. For others you simply want to mitigate them, or at least plan to absorb their negative effects.

Eliminating a risk generally means that you completely outsource the activity that leads to the risk or that you completely stop that activity. This, of course, generally means that the services of the nonprofit will be affected in some way. There are usually costs to risk management and eliminating a risk tends to be one of the more costly risk responses. Stopping an activity also involves costs, as it requires finding a new way of doing things, or to even cease providing a service that imposes a cost on the beneficiaries of the nonprofit. Occasionally, however, the need to search for a new method of doing things leads to more creative and better solutions.

Reducing an activity is not as drastic, but it too has costs in that it means that services will also likely be reduced. This is where being clear about the objectives of the nonprofit and the objectives of the risk management function become essential.

Mitigate

Mitigate is different from eliminating or reducing a risk, in that you still keep doing the activity that gives rise to the negative risk but you enact policies or procedures that reduce the probability of the risk occurring or reduce the impact if it does occur.

For instance, Rugby Nova Scotia is planning to implement enhanced training for all high school coaches. It is thought that better training will reduce injuries due to poorly executed tackles. The sport will still be played, and the risk of injury will still be present, so nothing in the sport is being eliminated or reduced, but the number of injuries, and the seriousness of the injuries will likely be reduced due to the mitigating factor of improved coaching.

Ignore

Some risks it is prudent to simply ignore. The risks may be too small, too improbable, or have too low of an impact to be meaningful. For other risks there is simply no way to practically control them.

Scrapes, bumps, and bruises in rugby are a prime example of a risk that one can ignore (beyond having readily available the elements of normal first aid basics for cleaning and dressing any wounds). If one chooses to play rugby without having a few scrapes and bruises, then one is better off choosing a different sport. There is no way to play rugby without running and tackling, which necessarily involves scrapes and bruises. The risk of a concussion, however, is a different matter and is a risk that absolutely should not be ignored.

Risks that are ignored should, however, be tracked in order to ensure that the nature of the risk is not changing, or that the nature of the risk was underestimated and is instead a risk that should instead be actively managed.

Enhance

Enhance is the good risk equivalent to mitigate for negative risk. Good risks can be enhanced by taking on more of the activity or by promoting the activity. For instance, Rugby Nova Scotia used the concern about the risk of injuries to promote the imposition of regulations to improve the quality of coaching. The suggestion is to require high school rugby coaches to obtain higher levels of certification.

Embrace

It seems counterintuitive, but risks can also be embraced, and not simply positive risks, but also negative risks. Embracing a risk means that the organization makes the risk one of the cores of their activities. The public outcry surrounding the suspension of high school rugby brought forward that the physicality of the sport instilled a culture of respect, discipline, and perhaps most importantly, self-esteem among participants. These are all very positive characteristics that can be used to promote and grow the sport. In other words, the very risk of the perceived physicality of the sport can be embraced to position the sport as a character builder for high school students. Combined with the other responses to the risk of injury such as a focus on coaching and adherence to rules, allows what was a negative risk to become a positive risk that can be leveraged for the good of the sport and its participants.

Concluding Thoughts

Before concluding this discussion on risk responses, it is important to realize that not every risk has a direct response available to it, except perhaps acceptance. Some risks the organization will simply have to accept. Some risks the organization will simply have no control over, and no way to performs actions that will shift either the impact or the probability of the risk occurring. These are the risks of being in operation. Unfortunately, the only way to manage them is to accept the risks, accept that there is no way to manage them, and to prepare for the worst and hope for the best. Contingency plans, and action plans for those instances when the risk becomes a reality is all that one can sometimes realistically do. That is the reality of risk management.

Fortunately for the vast majority of risks there are responses that an organization can undertake to manage them. These responses cover a wide range from eliminate to embrace. Risks can be managed internally, or they can be outsourced. Of course, the risks should be prioritized for risk management in the context of the organization's strategic objectives; not all risks are created equal, or of the same urgency and priority.

We believe that the critical point is that the organization considers its full range of responses before imposing what may with further analysis be perceived as a knee-jerk response. Developing new risk responses and risk tactics is an important part of being a risk-learning, and risk-wise organization.

The real-life case study of Nova Scotia high school rugby provides an interesting situation where a nonprofit school board makes a decision on some suspect relative risk data of rugby compared to other sports such as football and hockey. They initially decide to immediately cancel the rugby season just as the season was about to end. A diverse variety of stakeholders rallied and the provincial rugby association stepped in to allow the season to finish and for the board to outsource the management of the issue. It appears that the provincial rugby association will continue to administer high school rugby for the time being. Plans are for better coaching training and certification along with better training of referees. This will improve coaching and thus is expected to reduce injuries. The media attention brought to the matter has increased focus on the sport, potentially leading to greater participant by student athletes next year. Having high school students more active in physical fitness and sports has many well-recognized positive spin-offs.

Being fully aware of the full range of responses to risk makes risk management a much more valued activity. It makes risk management more effective, creates a better risk culture, and improves overall outcomes for the nonprofit.

CHAPTER 10

Partnerships and Stakeholder Engagement

The executive director of a (fictional) community resource center, Ms. Kathryn Lemay (Kathryn), was planning to propose a 1-day outdoor community fundraising event to her board. The center provided summer activities in the arts for underprivileged children. The center needed to have a strong reception to this annual fundraising event if it was to have any hope of continuing with their mandate in any meaningful manner. She knew that the board members were nonsupportive because of the problems they experienced the previous year.

Last year's event started poorly before it even began. They were not able to get permission from the city to use the city-owned facility until the last minute. Furthermore, support from the city was anemic at best. For instance, although the mayor was available, he refused to attend because he had some issues with two of the center's board members. Internally, support for the event was not much better. Staff complained about the unpaid overtime and the overload of their duties. Staff had to work more than what was planned because only few of the volunteers showed up, and those who did were uncertain about some of their duties. The catering company did not have enough food and beverages although the amount of people expected was clearly specified in their contract. The issue with the catering company would have been much worse if attendance had not been underwhelming. Even the weather was not cooperative as an unexpected shower during the children's dance routines, which was to be the centerpiece of the day, ruined it for all. Kathryn blamed herself for not checking the weather herself and arranging a weather contingency plan. Her assistant was supposed to do it but she unexpectedly resigned and moved to another nonprofit only 5 days before the event.

In terms of fundraising, it was a flop. Many of the donors who attended were not happy with overall quality of the event, nor the fact that it seemed to be so disorganized. It was demoralizing that so few of the children who were beneficiaries of the event were present, and of those that were, so few were actively involved. The community resource center spent nearly 20 percent of its events budget just for the promotion of the event. The aim was to raise at least 10 times more than what they invested but at the end of the day they just barely passed the breakeven point.

The following day Kathryn received 17 e-mails from different individuals complaining about different mishaps. Two of the four sponsors were complaining for not having enough exposure as they were told to expect. Some visitors were complaining about the quality of food and some others about the behavior of staff in addition to the fact that many of the children were not more involved. Three of the e-mails were from residents of the neighborhood complaining about the waste on streets that was not cleaned after the event and the noise level of the music.

The local media, including the local newspaper and representatives of a community TV show were also invited to the event. It was a big surprise for Ms. Kathryn when she saw the resulting coverage both on TV and in the newspaper. The focused on the chaos during the rain shower. The event lasted more than 5 hours but it seemed that they only showed the worst 5 minutes. Kathryn was disappointed and dispirited, but obviously she was not the only one.

This year though it was going to be different. Looking back on the previous summer's events, Kathryn took a deep breath and entered in the boardroom to meet with the planning committee to plan for the coming summer's event. The board members stopped chatting and stared at Kathryn. It was looking like it was starting out to be a tough meeting. In addition to the fiasco with the fundraising event, the new state government also decreased their funding by 30 percent. To compound matters, early donor contributions were also down by almost 50 percent from the same time last year. The success of this single fundraising activity would be even more critical than ever. This year though was going to be different. This year Kathryn had learned her lesson. This year she had a risk plan.

This is not a real story, but all nonprofit organizations experience similar troubles with their stakeholders. In many cases, the risks of nonprofit organizations are closely related with the stakeholders. The stakeholders are generally either part of the problem or part of the solution or at least have the potential to become a part of the problem or solution. The positive or negative contribution of the stakeholders depends on the nonprofit organizations' performance on managing stakeholder engagement and partnerships.

The Nature of Partnerships

We have seen many nonprofit board members and managers who spend significant part of their time to build strong partnerships with their stakeholders. If not in the short term, these efforts definitely pay back in the long term. On the contrary, those who ignore to invest the necessary time and energy on their stakeholders will very likely have trouble when they need external support to achieve their objectives.

Partnership risk management manifests itself in many ways. There are internal and external stakeholders. There are direct and indirect stakeholders. There are stakeholders that management has some influence or control over, and others, such as the weather, that they have no control over. Some partnerships are direct and contractual, such as vendors, and some are indirect and implicit such as neighbors. The point is that all partnerships need to be managed and nurtured. It is a risk management task that can make or break a nonprofit.

Stakeholder management begins with understanding the needs, desires, and objectives of the various partnerships. The diversity of the partnerships brings with it a diversity of objectives. Seldom are these objectives in alignment, and even rarer are they in complete alignment with the objectives of the nonprofit.

Imagine a case where a nonprofit organization has trouble to obtain funds from the local government because of the misalignments between their objectives. Consider that the city gives priority to charities that have services for youth, whereas the nonprofit organization offers services for poverty. In this example, the funding organization is part of the risk and the problem.

In such cases, nonprofit organizations have two options. Either they can adjust their strategies to fit with the objectives of the funding organization or they can try to convince funding organizations to change their objectives. The nonprofit organization can also try to implement both options simultaneously. If the nonprofit organization succeeds in finding a way to have the same objectives, the funding organizations may become part of the solution.

However, having similar objectives may not be enough to solve the problem and remove the risk. The funding organizations such as local governments will not provide funds to a nonprofit organization not only because they do not share the cause but also because they cannot see the value or impact of the services offered. Nonprofit organizations may not get funds even when they have similar objectives with the funding organizations, unless they convince the funders.

Partnership is the outcome of the process of making the stakeholders part of the solution. Successful nonprofit organizations use stakeholder engagement as a strategic tool to build strong partnerships to deal with risk. For example, Civica Rx, a massive hospital collaboration of more than 800 hospitals in the United States, demonstrated a good example of partnership. Its objective is to assure that essential generic medications are accessible and affordable. Civica Rx made an agreement with the Danish company Xellia Pharmaceuticals to produce vancomycin and daptomycin, two commonly used injectable antibiotics. The results were remarkable. Not only the prices went down, but the drugs were also available whenever they were needed.[1] This is a good example to show that partnership is possible even between competitors.

Vector Model

You must have seen or participated in tug-of-war game. In many management practices in the nonprofit sector we can observe similar cases. When different individuals or groups are not aligned in the same direction, they just cancel each other's strengths. Their energy and time is wasted.

However, when there are a diversity of stakeholders it gets more complicated than a two-way tug-of-war. It is more like a four-way tug-of-war

---

[1] https://nonprofitquarterly.org/massive-hospital-collaboration-based-nonprofit-bears-first-fruits/ (accessed July 22, 2019).

with the pulling being along two dimensions instead of just one. This is the basis of the vector model, which is illustrated in Figure 10.1.

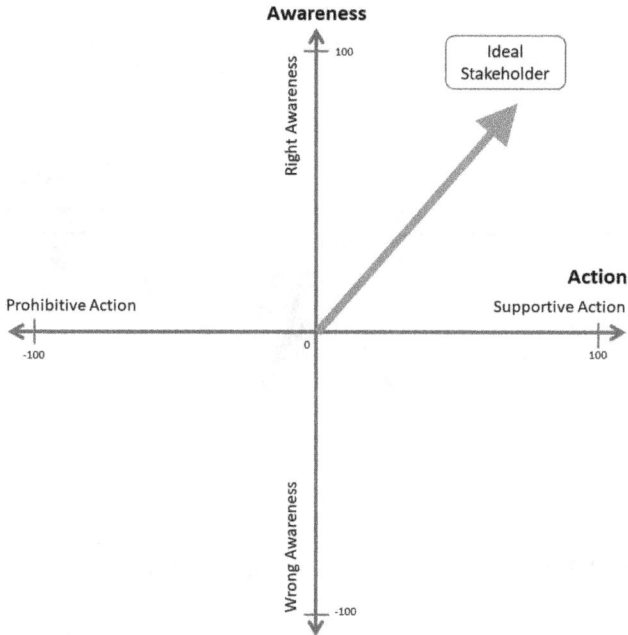

Figure 10.1 The vector model

We use the vector model as a metaphor to represent each team. If you are familiar with physics and mathematics, you will recall that vectors are quantities that have two independent properties: magnitude and direction, similar to the teams. In the vector model there are two dimensions; a dimension for action (which can be supportive or prohibitive) and a dimension for awareness (which can be positive or negative). The ideal stakeholder is one who has the proper awareness of the nonprofit and is supportive of their actions that support their objectives.

For almost every strategic or operational practice, you need to work against several other vectors with variable directions and magnitudes. We can use the same metaphor for the nonprofit stakeholders. Each stakeholder has a magnitude and direction, which may or may not support the nonprofit organization. Awareness and action can be used as two axes to measure and illustrate the vectors of stakeholders. Unless you assure that they are pulling in the same direction with you, it becomes a challenge to succeed as illustrated in Figure 10.2.

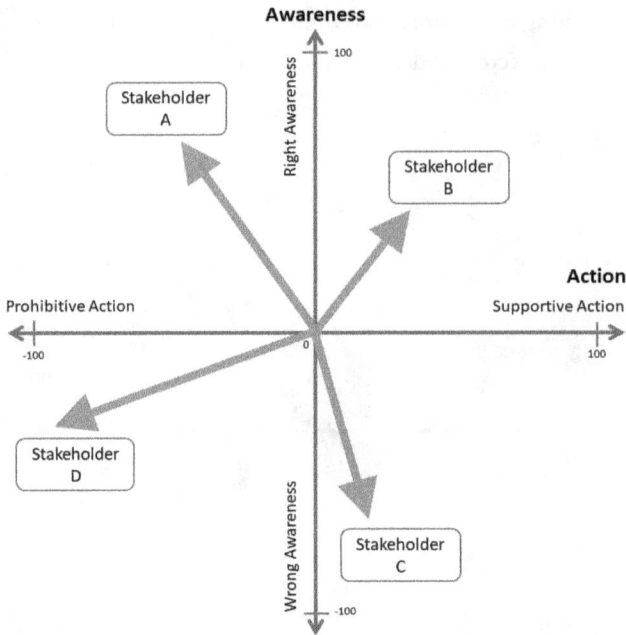

Figure 10.2 Vector model with competing stakeholders

As shown in the horizontal axis, stakeholders may have actions at different levels which will potentially support or prohibit the nonprofit organization. Similarly, the stakeholders may have right or wrong awareness about the objectives of the nonprofit organization or a particular decision. In an ideal case as illustrated in Figure 10.1, the stakeholder demonstrates the right awareness and supportive actions. This means perfect alignment with the nonprofit organization. Naturally, this will not be the case in many situations. Nonprofit organizations need to work with different stakeholders with different vectors. Figure 10.2 illustrates a possible case with four stakeholders. Without calculation, it is easy to see that the sum vector (the outcome of the situation) will be weak.

As a rule, diagnostics is the first and maybe the most significant step of treatment. If the nonprofit is aware of the vectors of its stakeholders than it can develop a strategy to bring all vectors in the same direction which can be addressed as stakeholder risk management as illustrated in Figure 10.3.

In a successful stakeholder management, the vectors of stakeholders will look like Figure 10.4. Although the vectors still have different

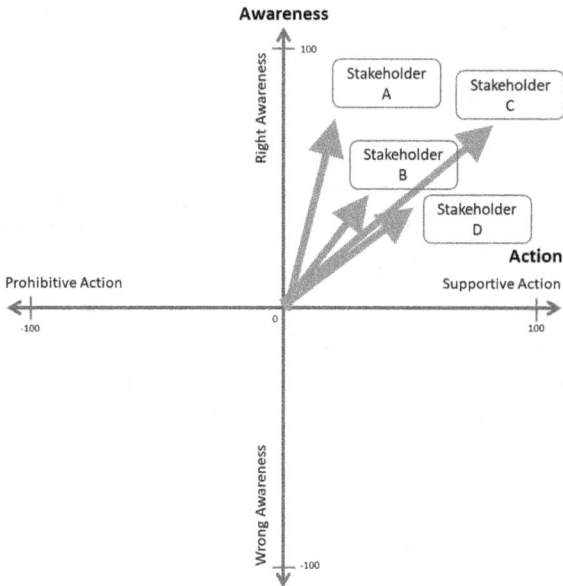

Figure 10.3 Alignment of stakeholders

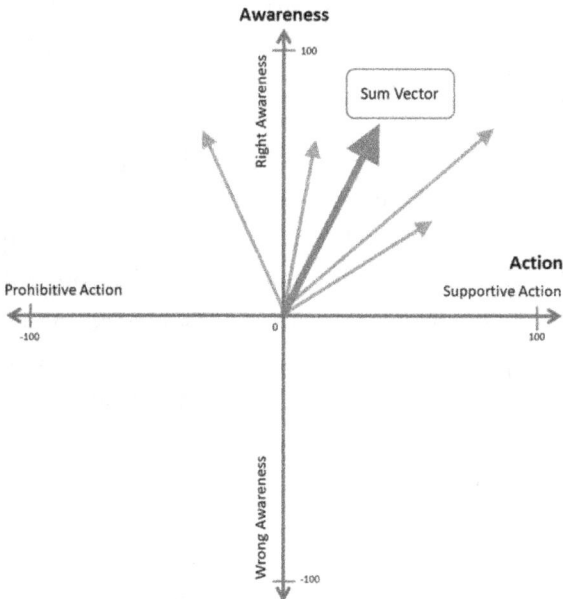

Figure 10.4 Alignment of stakeholders

magnitudes, they are all roughly in the same direction. This means they are not canceling each other's efforts. The sum vector will be bigger this time. Of course, this is an idealized situation. However, the greater the alignment, the better the stakeholder risk management will be. Admittedly, it generally takes a significant amount of persuasion, risk management and political skill to make it happen. Simply because members of the nonprofit are committed to their objectives, it does not necessarily follow that the stakeholders are committed to the same level, or even to the same objectives. Many nonprofit organization managers assume that their objectives are clear and all stakeholders have the same understanding. Especially for well-known nonprofit services such as food banks, human shelters, hospitals, or training centers objectives may seem obvious. However, this may not be the case.

For a food bank, for example, some people may think that having more food for more people is the objective, whereas the management team focuses on more healthy food. This tiny difference can scale up when it comes to alignment and cause risk and conflict.

In Pittsburgh, a nonprofit organization named the Manchester Bidwell Corporation ("Bidwell"), which has spawned a model linking the arts, technology, and workforce development, was offered 22 acres of public land by Pennsylvania for the price of $1. This land transfer decision to Bidwell upset community leaders in Pittsburgh because the community did not share the objectives of Bidwell.[2]

Another risk related to stakeholders may be about the way of operations. There was discussion about the impact of human shelter services in a well-known Canadian charity. Some board members argued that their services were helpful for homeless people in the short run. However others argued that unlimited shelter services prevent homeless people from moving forward in their lives. In this case, there was a common understanding about "what needs to be done" but there was no agreement on "how."

Once all vectors are aligned approximately in the same direction, the nonprofit stakeholder management team can focus on the magnitudes.

---

[2]https://nonprofitquarterly.org/proposed-land-transfer-to-nonprofit-in-pittsburgh-upsets-community-leaders/ (accessed July 22, 2019).

This will require more awareness and more supportive action. Better communication is one of the tools that can be used. Nonprofit organizations can also adjust their strategies to align with their stakeholders. This means, for the sake of solidarity, that nonprofit organization should not only try to change their stakeholders but also adjust their own practices whenever appropriate. It will generally necessitate a series of compromises.

This approach can be used both at the operational and the strategic level, and the results may be different. It should not be a surprise because the stakeholders of a nonprofit organization may be different both at the operational and the strategic level. Each level and each stakeholder have to be managed separately as illustrated in Figure 10.5. It will require time and effort but is critical not only for risk mitigation but also for the overall success of the nonprofit organization.

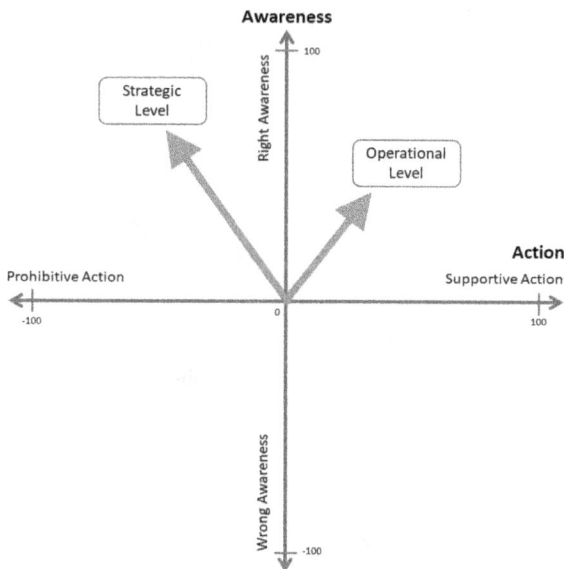

Figure 10.5 Strategic and operational alignment

The vector model can also be used as a strategic tool in nonprofit organizations. As illustrated in Figure 10.6, the decision team can compare the measured (current) and aimed sum vectors that will enable the nonprofit organization to develop necessary actions to achieve its goal.

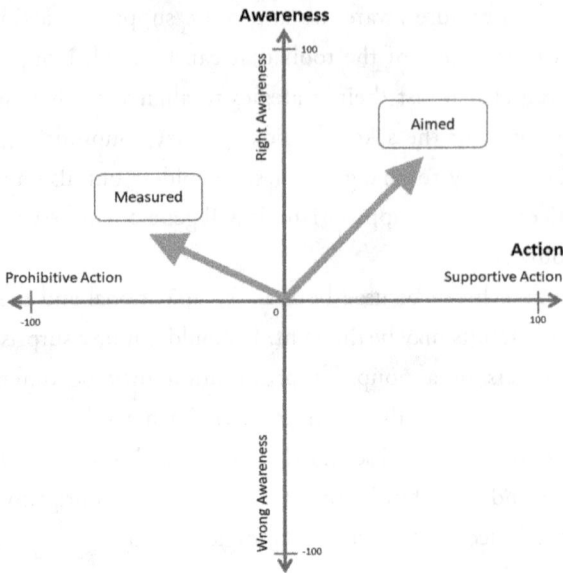

Figure 10.6 *Measured versus aimed for vectors*

Stakeholder Trio

It is instructive to return to the stakeholder trio that was introduced in Chapter 3 as part of the risk management tower. In the framework, replicated in Figure 10.7, we propose to categorize stakeholders in three groups: service providers, sponsors and regulators, and beneficiaries.

The first group of the nonprofit stakeholder trio is "the service providers." Service providers include staff members and volunteers as well as partnering organizations and individuals for the delivery of the services.

The second group is "the sponsors" and they include governments, funding organizations and donors that assist the nonprofit organization financially or in another format. Regulators would include national and local governments, national and international regulatory organizations, and social institutes that have formal or informal control over the actions of the nonprofit organization. Since in many cases funding organizations also regulate the nonprofit's domain, we preferred to have them in the same category.

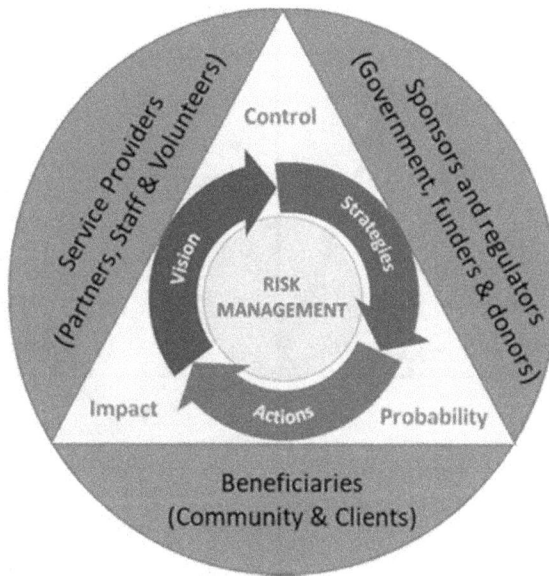

Figure 10.7 Stakeholder trio

Finally, the last but not least group of the nonprofit trio is "the benefi-ciaries." It includes both individuals that directly benefit from the services or community members that indirectly benefit from the services. For ex-ample, the clients of a nonprofit employment support center will directly benefit from the services when they get assistance to find a job. Their families will also benefit from the services but indirectly. We categorize all direct and indirect beneficiaries under the same group.

We can use vector model to illustrate different stakeholders as in Figure 10.8. The flexibility of the model enables the nonprofit organiza-tions to use it for their specific needs with minor customization.

The measurements of vectors does not have to be done professionally by researchers or expert consultants. The nonprofit management team can also roughly measure the vectors of each stakeholder based on the observations. Even in that case the graphs will provide useful information for decision makers to use stakeholder engagement as a risk management tool. It clearly illustrates though that when used for the management of stakeholder trio, the nonprofit organization will likely need to develop different engagement strategies for each group.

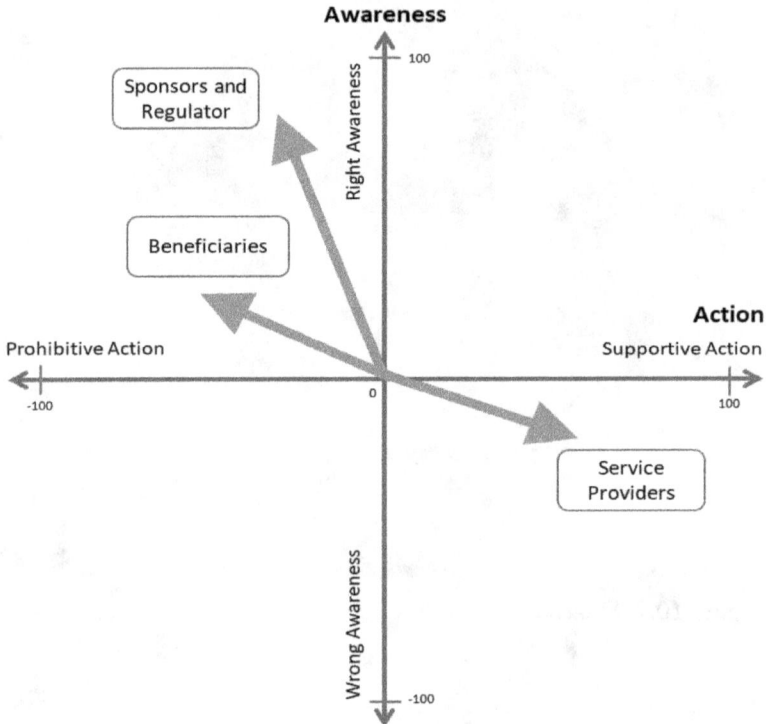

Figure 10.8 Stakeholder diversity and the vector model

Stakeholder Risks

Each group of stakeholders present different kinds of stakeholder risks. We have already discussed strategic and alignment risks at length, but there are also major financial, operational, legal, and reputational risks. As previously mentioned, this is compounded by the fact that many stakeholder risks are external and thus beyond the direct control of the managers of the nonprofit.

Stakeholder risk management first begins with communication; communication both internally of dealing with stakeholders as well as communication with each of the stakeholder constituencies themselves. Part of communication management is being clear about the message, and part of communication management is being clear about who has accountability for managing each of the various stakeholders.

To ensure consistency in messaging, it is often helpful to have a stakeholder statement prepared that should be part of a mandatory distribution to all key stakeholders. The stakeholder statement should include facts about the mission of the nonprofit and clearly spell out expectations about conduct of the stakeholders when they are acting as either an agent, representative or as a supplier to the nonprofit. Although the conduct of stakeholders is often beyond the direct control of the nonprofit, the reality is that inappropriate behavior by a stakeholder will generally be attributed to the nonprofit, regardless of the amount of control that the nonprofit could reasonably be expected to have over the stakeholder. Reputation risk by mere association is very real. It can be managed for a positive risk, or left unmanaged, it can easily turn into a disastrous negative risk with long-term consequences.

It is useful to identify and plot the significant stakeholder risks as part of the risk mapping exercise discussed in Chapter 5. Once the stakeholder risks are identified, it is then possible to develop a risk management plan just as one would for any other type of risk. Again, it is important to realize that each stakeholder will bring their own portfolio of risks.

The one thing that the nonprofit should strive to do is to at least manage the stakeholder risks that are under their control. These include the risks associated with employees and staff (both paid employees as well as volunteers), board members, and managers. It reflects very poorly if unnecessary risks are brought onto the nonprofit through internal neglect.

For external stakeholders, such as suppliers and donors, flexibility, slack, and contingency plans need to be developed. As with all risks, external stakeholders should be viewed as risks that could be positive or negative. Just as external stakeholders can create negative risks simply by association, they can also create opportunities for positive outcomes by association.

The diversity of stakeholders implies that the organization should strive to have a diversity of managers, staff, and board members who also have diversity in terms of their connections. For instance, a diverse board will be able to create external connections with stakeholders, improving relations, improving communication, and by extension improving stakeholder risk management.

Revisiting Katheryn's Situation

Before concluding this chapter, let's take a moment to review the hypothetical situation that we began the chapter with. To recap, Katheryn Lemay, the director for a nonprofit that provided summer arts activities for underprivileged children had previously experienced a disastrous fundraising event in which there were a number of mishaps with a variety of stakeholders. Among the issues were the fundraiser barely broke even putting a crimp on next year's budget which was made even worse by a cut in state funding; there were too few volunteers and those that did show appeared to be uncertain what their roles were to be, while the person responsible for many of the operational details resigned 5 days before the event; permissions to use a city-owned facility were late in being granted and neighbors complained about the noise and the debris left behind; donors who attended were disappointed by the number of beneficiary children who participated in the event; the food vendor did not deliver enough food and the food that was delivered was not of the quality expected; news coverage of the event was negative and put the nonprofit's organizational abilities into question; and just to cap things off, it rained during the centerpiece event of the afternoon which threw the entire event into chaos. In summary the event was a mess. To prevent a repeat fiasco, it is instructive to think of some of the risk management steps in regards to stakeholders that Kathryn might take.

Planning a major fundraiser is obviously a project management exercise and exercising best practice in project management will definitely aid in the risk management process. Likewise, risk management can also significantly aid project management. It is a reciprocal relationship. Risk management should thus be designed in parallel with project management. In an ideal situation, risk management would be completely integrated with the project management process.

The first step in risk management of this situation would be to develop a risk map. As there are a wide variety of stakeholders involved in such an event, it may be useful to have a separate risk map just for them. The risk map would identify the stakeholders who would be a priority for risk management, and also point out those for which the organization would have differing levels of control as it would relate to the risk management issues. Prioritization helps manage the scarce time resources of the center's staff, and understanding the levels of controls indicates those stakeholders for whom contingency plans, extra buffers or other management plans may be needed to account for the lack of control.

A communication strategy could also be developed and implemented for each of the major stakeholders. One of the issues in Kathryn's hypothetical example was that it appeared that there were several assumptions of how others would view their role in the event. For instance, volunteers were uncertain of their role, they appeared to be uncertain of how many were needed, and it also was not impressed on the children who were the beneficiaries of the nonprofit how important their involvement would be.

In addition to a pre-event communication strategy, a post-event communication strategy could be preplanned to manage any possible reputational risk that may exist after such an event. Again, it would be important to emphasize that this could be a positive risk just as probable as it could be a negative risk. If things go better than expected, the nonprofit should not delay taking advantage of that in its communication with relevant stakeholders.

The communication strategy would also lead to an awareness of the competing agendas of the various stakeholders. Political issues between the mayor and board members could have possibly been uncovered, an awareness of what donors wanted to experience at the event could have been clarified and subsequently planned for, and potential issues with affected neighbors could have been more effectively managed.

From the communication strategy, accountability for managing the risks related to the various stakeholders could have been assigned. While the director needs to oversee and manage the event (as well as all of the other ongoing operations of the nonprofit), there simply are too many facets for a single director to manage not only all of the operational details but also the risk management details. Risk management tasks, and in particular risk management of the stakeholders in such a situation needs to be delegated with clear indications of who is accountable for which set of risks and stakeholder relationships.

It should not take a fiasco to highlight the importance of risk management, and in particular stakeholder risk management. Doing the basics of risk management for stakeholder risks, such as risk mapping, will greatly enhance stakeholder relationships. A few common-sense steps in risk management, would have saved Kathryn a lot of trouble and greatly increased the probability of more positive outcomes.

Concluding Thoughts

Managing stakeholder risks is tricky. They are diverse, there is often limited levers of control, and they can be quite unpredictable. Organizations often do not know as much as they would like about their stakeholders, which adds to the unpredictability. Furthermore, many of the stakeholder risks may be hidden or difficult to ascertain a priori. Stakeholders and partners can affect the organization both directly and indirectly. They can even affect the organization by association.

Being aware of the diversity of stakeholder risks, and explicitly including them as part of the risk management plan is key. Depending on the nature of the organization, it may be worthwhile to have a separate risk management planning session to deal with the portfolio of stakeholder risks by themselves.

Stakeholders often seem to be considered to be secondary to the operations of the nonprofit. Our experience tells us that thinking so is a major risk management mistake. Stakeholders are key to almost every nonprofit. If treated in a risk-intelligent manner, stakeholders can be a valuable risk-positive asset.

CHAPTER 11

Risk Governance

Just like many of you, we enjoy traveling by car during our vacations as a family. We feel more flexible when compared to a bus tour. Depending on the length of the trip, we frequently exchange seats; however, I am usually the one who drives the car. I drive the car, but this does not necessarily mean that we go to the places I decide. All family members make the decisions together, usually with consensus. Our simple family tradition can teach us the difference between management and governance: driving the car is management, whereas deciding where to go and monitoring the performance of the driver is governance.

In contrast to the simplicity of the definitions, if not implemented properly the management-governance confusions have the potential to generate complex problems in nonprofit organizations. Referring back to our family car metaphor, it is easy to conclude that the executive director of a nonprofit organization is the driver of the nonprofit organization, whereas board members are the travelers who make the decisions.

Having clear and respected boundaries between governance and management is critical in nonprofit organizations. If the board members interfere with the managerial tasks this may have detrimental consequences. Similarly, if the executive director of the nonprofit organization uses too much initiative and ignores to follow board guidance the outcomes may be destructive. Likewise, it is true that senior management must also respect the delegation of authority and accountability of the appropriate parts of risk management to the relevant staff and employees.

The literature for governance for all types of organizations is extensive. While our focus is on the specific aspects of risk governance, there are several general governance principles that need to be clearly understood. It is important to be aware of the fact that the governance and the management are two different functions of nonprofit organizations. There may be some similarities and overlaps, however, board members and management teams of nonprofit organizations need to practice these two functions separately. This does not mean there will be no interaction or collaboration. On the contrary, when boundaries are clear there will be more room for collaboration

Managing Boundaries

The conceptual distinction between management and governance may sound easy; however, real-life implementation is always a challenge and holds risks for the nonprofit. The following process of boundary management, illustrated in Figure 11.1, is crucial to mitigate any risks related to the confusion of roles.

Figure 11.1 Boundary management

The first step of the process is boundary setting and addresses the clear identification of the management and the governance roles. A written explanation of board and executive director roles is a good way to create a formal boundary setting.

The second step is the communication of boundaries. As highlighted in this book several times, the primary source of risk in nonprofit organizations is the human factor. If nonprofit organizations communicate the boundaries both with board members and with management teams properly it will avoid many risks that will appear if not done this way.

Finally, the last but not least step of the boundary management is the boundary control. Both parties need to respect the boundaries and behave accordingly. In case of any crossovers, either the board or the executive director (or both) have to detect the intrusions and intruders immediately and warn related individuals in a proper way. This may be a difficult conversation but, compared with the outcomes of ignored breaches, it is preferable.

Shifting Boundaries

Even when we carefully follow the three steps of boundary management, we may still face risks that can be caused by the changes in the conditions. In a healthy and stable nonprofit organization, the responsibilities at the normative, the strategic, and the operational level will look something similar to the drawing in Figure 11.2.

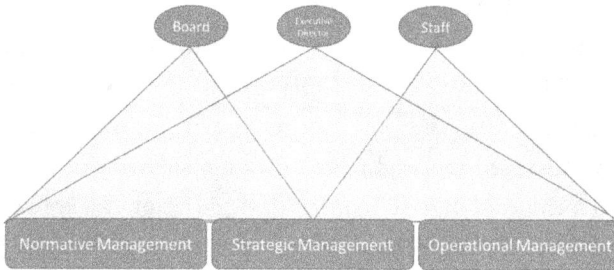

Figure 11.2 Separation of duties

Be aware that the overlaps do not indicate tasks but responsibilities. The board should fulfill its responsibilities with guidance and performance monitoring whereas the executive director will utilize the management tools.

On a highway with light traffic, as the default driver of my family during vacations, I do not need much guidance. What I need to do is simple and obvious. While I drive the car, other members of my family can enjoy the nice view with minimum involvement. When we enter a city, they immediately change their attitudes and become more focused on the directions. Even finding the best parking spot becomes a family decision.

This example illustrates that the management and the governance roles may change and shift based on the external conditions and other factors. During certain periods, nonprofit organizations can expect board members to be more involved with decisions. Similarly, during certain periods the board may prefer to give more flexibility and initiative to the nonprofit management teams.

As far as the board and the executive directors manage the boundary shifts properly, the dynamic boundaries are not challenges or risk sources for the organization. Contrarily, having an adaptive governance structure may be a useful risk mitigation tool.

In addition to the board and executive directors, other staff members may also be involved in governance at certain level. Managers of particular services or field experts of unique subjects can temporarily assist the governance of the nonprofit organization. Formal structures and written policies will make these incidents less risky.

Hierarchy of Risk Governance

It is natural for nonprofit boards and staff to each have a different focus. They have different functions, and they are also privy to different sets of information and awareness. The staff responsible for the delivery of the services are expected to spend more time on operational issues, whereas the board members will focus more on strategic factors. Figure 11.3 summarizes the roles of different members of nonprofit organizations.

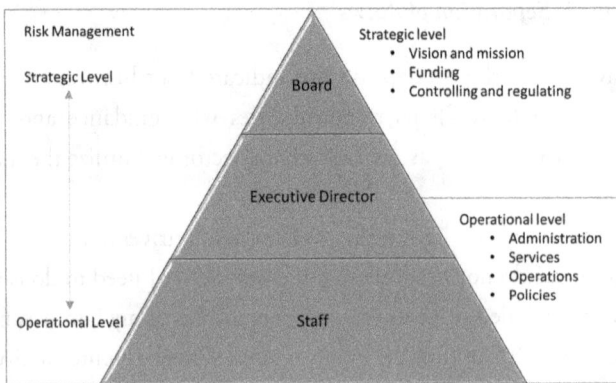

Figure 11.3 Hierarchy of risk governance

Not only the type but also the components of the risk will change based on the hierarchical level. As someone can expect, the board will focus more on risks that potentially have more impact on the organization, whereas staff members generally deal with low-impact risks.

In terms of the control of the risk, we usually have an opposite condition. At the strategic level, the level of control over the risk becomes less. For example, imagine a nonprofit organization that considers losing data as a risk. To avoid any loss of data, the nonprofit organization can install a data backup system that will significantly mitigate the risk. Consider another case where the nonprofit organization is concerned about the potential cuts in government funds because of a change in government priorities. Although it is a very impactful risk, the board has almost no control over it.

The third factor of risk is the probability, which is not related with the hierarchical level of the risk. The likelihood of any risk is independent from its level. Figure 11.4 gives a brief idea about the hierarchy of risk in nonprofit organization. This information is important to form the risk governance system in a nonprofit organization.

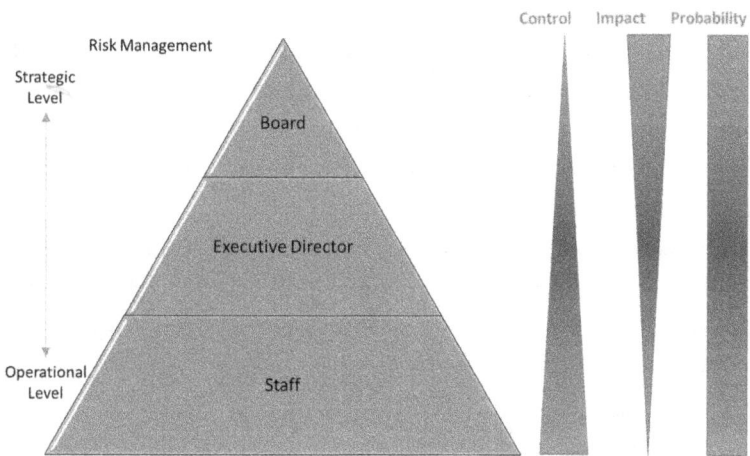

Figure 11.4 Hierarchy of risk

Specific Risk Activities

There are a variety of specific risk management activities that the board should play an active part in. The first and primary one is that the board members themselves need risk training and awareness. In the for-profit sector, there has been a concerted effort to increase board members risk knowledge over the last decades. For most board members of publicly traded companies, specific risk training has become almost universally mandatory. Additionally, most for-profit organizations will have a special working committee of the board that focuses solely on risk management. This was a major component of the various risk frameworks that were discussed in Chapter 3. The need for risk training, however, may be even greater for board members of nonprofits. A board cannot provide proper oversight and impose good risk governance if they do not have the knowledge or the training to understand properly the issues.

Proper risk training for the board will generally be of a quite different nature than the risk training for the staff, or even the risk training necessary for managers. Board members will not be implementing or managing the risk plan, but instead will be overseeing it. Board risk training should be designed with this in mind.

The training should focus on the key activities of risk governance and include: risk communication; understanding of issues surrounding risk tolerance and risk appetite; awareness of major risk metrics and especially those involved in the creation of risk dashboards; risk identification, mapping and prioritization; and finally training to appreciate the value of effective risk management.

Our experience has been that nonprofit board members are asked to serve based more on a specific operational expertise, such as finance or legal expertise, or, in contrast, based on their interest and background with the activities of the nonprofit. Rarely are board members asked to serve based on their risk management expertise. With this being the case, a little bit of risk management training can be a significant help to both new and existing board members.

Set Objectives for Risk Management

It has been stressed throughout the book that risk management is to serve the objectives of the organization. That should be, by far, the primary objective of the risk management function. However, there may be other specific objectives that the board may want to set for risk management. Among many things, these objectives might include improving the reputation of the organization, improving financial risk, satisfying the risk requirements of a regulator or potential partner, or improving prospects for external funding.

As part of its strategy setting function, the board should also pay some attention to setting a strategic risk management set of objectives. Furthermore, these objectives should be revisited on a periodic basis.

As part of its overall oversight role, the board should ensure that the risk management activities are achieving the objectives set out for it. If not, management should be tasked with amending the risk management implementation to create closer alignment with the risk management goals. This may seem like such an obvious statement that it does not merit mentioning. However, we have frequently observed that the risk management function, without oversight from the board, takes on a life of its own and becomes a bureaucratic drag on the efficiency of the organization. Conversely, without board oversight, the risk management activities may be given a low priority or even allowed to lapse entirely. Periodic oversight to ensure alignment with set objectives will help prevent this from happening.

Set Risk Tolerance and Appetite

Perhaps the most crucial function of the board is to set the risk tolerance and the risk appetite of the firm as previously discussed in Chapter 3. To recap, the risk tolerance are those risks that the organization will not take or will avoid at all reasonable levels. The risk appetite, however, is the overall level of risk that the organization will be comfortable operating with. Both risk tolerance and risk appetite are strategic risk issues and thus should be set by the board, which should also have ongoing oversight.

For many organizations, setting the risk tolerance is relatively straightforward; there is an obvious and general agreement on the risks that should not be tolerated. For other types of organizations, it can be a highly nuanced task. To reiterate, it is generally not possible to eliminate risk. Thus, the risk tolerance cannot ever be set with surety. The board sets this level of risk tolerance or creates a list of risks that the organization will do all that they can to avoid. This may imply that some activities of the organization may have to be significantly altered, or even discontinued.

It is important to note that different organizations, even those that have similar missions, may have very different levels of risk tolerance. For instance, two youth soccer leagues may have a different tolerance around concussions. One league may impose a concussion protocol and awareness program in an attempt to minimize the probability and severity of concussions but not put concussions in its risk tolerance category. Another youth soccer league, however, may decide that concussions are not tolerable and thus change their rules so that heading the ball is banned. Either decision in this example is likely to spark an impassioned debate among stakeholders.

Set the Risk Management Tone

The board, in close partnership with management, can also play a critical role in setting the tone and risk culture of the organization. In particular, it can help by making it known that risk is a natural part of any organization. The board can help to communicate that risk management is taken seriously and is being used to more efficiently and effectively manage the organization and serve its beneficiaries. The board can set the tone that risk management is not to be viewed as a needless level of bureaucracy or as a methodology to find fault but as a strategic tool to help everyone throughout the organization.

Too often risk management is implemented as a negative. Risk management can be seen as such for a variety of reasons. The first and primary is that as previously discussed, risk is defined by most people as the possibility that something bad can happen. A second reason is that risk management is often only implemented in an organization after something bad *has* happened. This only puts a negative tone around the risk management function. If risk management is implemented proactively, it can be positioned as a positive. It is this message, and this tone, that the board can play a major part in setting.

Accidents and inadvertent risk mistakes should not be perceived as instances for punishment but instead as instances for learning. If the board sets a tone for a healthy risk culture, then the risk culture is likely to be not only healthier but also more effective.

Board members need to be aware that their personal actions help to set the tone as well. Board members are sometimes public figures. If they are performing actions that may harm the reputation of the nonprofit, or are contradictory to the tone that they state they are trying to set within the nonprofit, then the tone that will be set will likely be one of cynicism among the management and staff. This is true even if such actions are performed in duties that are remote from the nonprofit itself. Board members not only have to "talk the talk" but must also "walk the walk" in their actions both as agents within and as agents removed from the nonprofit.

Risk Communication

One significant component of risk governance is the risk communication. The transfer of risk information between the board, the executive director, and staff is critically important for the development and implementation of proper actions. It is the board's responsibility to ensure that it, as well as management, is getting the right risk information in a timely manner.

In terms of risk communication, we focus on three internal and three external situations. Internal risk communication situations are as follows:

1. **Bottom-up risk communication:** In this case, the operational level staff members of the nonprofit organization identifies and detects the risk and informs the upper management levels when there is a need.

2. **Top-down risk communication:** Second case is a situation where the board or the executive director initiates the process. The risk information is transferred to the staff through the executive directors and other middle-class managers.

3. **Horizontal risk communication:** Such risk communication happens where different departments of a nonprofit organization exchange risk information at horizontal level. The horizontal risk communication can go directly or through top managers.

External risk communication situations are as follows:

1. **Narrow transmission:** In narrow transmission, the nonprofit management communicates the identified risks with a selected limited number of stakeholders. For example, a charity that forecasts financial risks can communicate financial risks with its financial partners including its funders, major donors, and financial institutes.

2. **Broad transmission:** When the risk is relevant to all stakeholders, the nonprofit organization may prefer to communicate risk publicly. A charity who offer immigrant integration services for Syrian refugees may make a public announcement about their risks after the general announcement of the government that forecasts ten times more refugees in the following 2 years. Since all stakeholders are one

way or another related to the solution, a broad transmission may be more practical.

3. **Receiving:** In this scenario, the nonprofit organization prefers to listen rather than posting any risk messages. It interprets stakeholder messages to foresee risks. For example, following governmental meetings to learn more about government cuts is a good example of receiving mode.

Risk Dashboard Design

To make sure that it is properly abreast of risk issues, the board should design a risk dashboard that will be presented to them at each of their meetings. As discussed in Chapter 5, the risk dashboard should provide an easy-to-understand set of key metrics that help the board answer the question of whether the organization is operating at appropriate risk levels.

The risk dashboard is a critical tool for the board to understand and appreciate how the organization is doing in its risk management activities. Obviously, board members do not have the time to check in on, or even appreciate the myriad risk management activities going on. That is why design of the risk dashboard is so critical.

It is important to note that the risk dashboard for the board is not necessarily the same as the risk dashboard for executives or others in the organization. Each level of governance will have their own dashboards that reflect the risk objectives that they are following and that they are accountable for.

Designing a risk dashboard for board members is not trivial. It requires a clear understanding of the risk objectives, creativity in design so it can be easily understood and interpreted, and thoughtfulness in how to measure and capture the data required to make a proper risk assessment.

Escalation for Critical Situations

The fuel level indicators on the dashboards of your car is a good metaphor to explain how the hierarchy of risk works. When the tank is half-full or more, the staff members of the nonprofit organization can handle the risk. When the fuel level is under half the executive director will be involved.

Finally, if the fuel level is in the last quarter the board will be involved because if the car is out of gas it may have severe consequences. As the final warning, the car dashboards have fuel warning lights. They turn on to warn drivers to replenish as soon as possible (Figure 11.5).

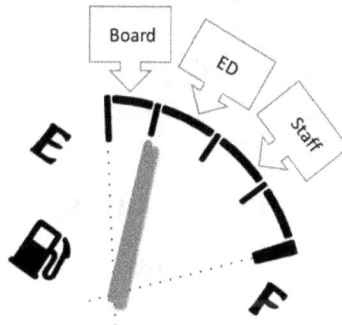

Figure 11.5 Escalation dashboard

In a similar way, when things get critical in terms of a risk event, that is when the issue should be escalated to the board. The board should be quite clear about when and how risks should be escalated. Both quantitative and qualitative measures should be used to ensure there is no ambiguity about escalation. There should be a clear and easy manner in which anyone in the organization can escalate an appropriate critical risk.

An important additional consideration is protection for "whistleblower." No one wants to be the deliverer of bad news. Often, there may be implications (real or perceived) for those who escalate critical issues. In the for-profit context this has led to the development of whistleblower laws that protect those who escalate the wrong doings of others. A similar protection for "risk whistleblowers" should be instituted. Without such a policy, there is an increased probability of issues not getting escalated in a timely manner due to the nature of people to try to hinder or procrastinate when it comes to dealing with negative news.

Sounding-Board for Management

The board as a whole is a sounding-board for management. It is only natural that the board should also be a sounding-board for risk management. The experience and diversity inherent in a well-formed board can provide valuable advice and feedback on risk management issues even without specific risk management expertise.

As part of assisting in the sounding-board role, board members may be invited to participate in implementing the steps of the risk framework and the risk management strategy as a whole. For instance, participation of board members in a risk identification, a risk mapping, or a risk prioritization exercise can significantly enhance the ability of the board to interact and advise management on risk tactics.

Symptoms of Ineffective Risk Governance

Perhaps it is easiest to explain good risk governance through the characteristics and symptoms of ineffective risk governance. The first major symptom of ineffective risk governance is the risk culture of the organization. If staff and volunteers are afraid to execute their tasks for fear of making a mistake, or fear of being blamed for making a mistake, then that is a telling sign of a poor risk culture and poor risk governance. The board needs to set, communicate, and insure the maintenance of the risk culture of the organization. Failure to do so is poor risk governance.

A second sign of poor risk governance is lack of well-defined goals for the risk management function. If the overall goals of the risk function are not widely known and understood, then governance is lacking. Likewise, if everyone in the organization does not know what risk management activities that they are responsible for, and perhaps more importantly why they are responsible for those risks, then there is poor risk governance.

Thirdly an organization with poor risk governance will also exhibit signs of poor risk communication. If board members and managerial staff are not able to quickly and easily explain whether the organization is improving or regressing in its risk management activities, and back that assessment up with appropriate data, then there is a deficiency in risk communication which implies a deficiency in risk governance. This is particularly true for risk dashboard items. If the key metrics for risk management are not known, or the data for assessment are not available, then there are risk governance issues in communication.

To conclude, perhaps the most basic as well as the most telling characteristic of ineffective risk governance is that the organization exhibits poor management overall. Management and risk management are intricately joined. If an organization exhibits poor management then it almost certainly has poor risk governance. Likewise, if the organization exhibits poor risk governance, then it most likely has poor management.

Concluding Thoughts

The board of a nonprofit plays an important role in many ways. Governance of risk management is one of those important roles. The board obviously cannot manage the day-to-day functions of risk management for the nonprofit. It is thus important to set clear boundaries for accountability and responsibility when it comes to risk management.

Ultimately good governance is good risk governance. We view risk management as an integral part of management. Just as governance is important to good management, so is risk governance important to risk management.

CHAPTER 12

The Future of Risk Management

Obviously, no one can accurately forecast the future. However, when it comes to risk management, there are some trends that give some strong clues as to what the future for risk management might hold. These trends have significance as well for nonprofits. In particular, there are two major and related trends that we see having the most impact on risk management for the nonprofit organization. These two significant trends are the increasing impact of technology, and an increasing level of complexity. In turn, these two trends are creating risk trends of increasing speed of risk management, shorter time frames for reliable risk forecasting, increasing importance of stakeholder management, and an increasing level of collaboration as well as competition for nonprofits.

Technology and Risk

Just as technology is changing our daily lives, so too is technology changing risk management. Four major technology themes are at the forefront of risk management: (1) the Internet of Things, (2) social media, (3) machine learning, and (4) fintech. In addition to changing how organizations conduct their day-to-day operations, these four technologies are changing the pace of change in risk management as well as the expectations for risk management. These technologies are creating exciting opportunities for nonprofits not only to improve the efficiencies of their operations but also to dramatically improve their risk management. Conversely, these technologies are also creating extra challenges for managers to manage and new levels of expectations for risk management.

The Internet of Things (IoT), facilitated by Internet-connected devices, is creating a flood of real-time data that can be used for risk management. IoT has already dramatically changed supply chain management as everyone can now track their Internet purchases in real time through stages of production on to stages of delivery. This same technology and way of thinking can also be used to track and record real-time risks.

For instance, sports injuries can be tracked in real time using body sensors. The club football team at Dalhousie University in Canada has purchased IoT-enabled "smart" football helmets that allow coaches and trainers to track impacts in real time. The sensors provide data that alerts the sidelines when a player has suffered a hit that was significant enough to cause a concussion.[1] This allows the trainers to take a player out of the game for assessment before potential further injury. It also takes the decision out of the hands of the player themselves as to whether or not they are in a condition to continue playing. This is significant as the player is often not in a state of mind that allows for them to make an accurate assessment.

While this is perhaps a unique example, examples in other areas abound. Body and dashboard cameras, driving habit recorders, warehouse shelf scanners, and loyalty cards tracking patrons are just a few of the common examples of IoT currently being used for risk management purposes. The instances of use for risk management of the IoT are limitless. It also comes with some considerations. First off is the management of the data. Having more data is great, but if it is not used effectively, it can do more harm than good. Also, the amount of data can be overwhelming. Designing good risk dashboards, and careful risk prioritization, becomes ever more critical as the amount of data available increases.

The increase of data also creates information technology data risk. Data risk has been previously discussed in several places already, but it bears repeating as we discuss the future of risk management. Data is the driver behind technology, and technology is driving the future of risk management as we envision it.

---

[1]https://globalnews.ca/news/5216204/dalhousie-university-smart-helmets-football/ (accessed July 6, 2019).

The upside of data risk is the numerous enhanced possibilities for risk management that it allows. The downside is the equally numerous negative risks that it brings. Data poses not only security risks but also a host of ethical risks. As previously mentioned, data risk is sophisticated and many of the issues may be beyond the experience level of managers of nonprofits who do not specialize in it. The inexperience with data risks has two sides to it: technical expertise in how to deal with it, and experience in how to recognize embedded data risks themselves.

Issues such as data security are coming to the fore. Society is slowly becoming aware of the downsides of having too much of their personal data exposed. Demands are being placed on all types of organizations not only to secure the data but also to be certain not to use the data in an unwarranted or unauthorized manner. Big Data, combined with machine learning can lead to lots of unintended consequences such as people being denied insurance or experiencing a form of unintended bias. We predict that the issues of what data is collected, how the data is used, and the security of the data will continue to increase in importance.

The flood of data is also accelerating due to the ubiquitous nature of social media. Events are being recorded, promoted, and shared on a continuous basis. Furthermore, events are being shared often without proper context. The reputational risks of this have already been discussed but bear repeating. With social media, it means that someone is always watching, and that any significant news can be quickly and widely shared.

Social media is also a valuable tool for the nonprofit to get their message out and to build a community. Social media is a powerful marketing tool that many organizations have come to rely on. It increases the breath of impact greatly for those nonprofits that choose to use the various platforms to do so. It allows nonprofits a variety of ways to make connections with their stakeholders and to build their profile.

Social media is a trend that exhibits both the upside and downside natures of risk. As discussed in Chapter 8, social media is a trend that needs to be actively managed for risk management purposes. However, few nonprofits that we are aware of think of social media as both a tool and a threat that requires active risk management.

The torrent of data provided by social media and by IoT is giving rise to the use of machine learning for risk management. As the amount of

data becomes humanly unmanageable, the task of data analysis and interpretation is increasingly becoming the domain of computers or bots. For
instance, it is estimated that the number of automobile fatalities could
be reduced by as much as 95 percent by a complete changeover to autonomous vehicles.[2] This is an amazing example of the power of machine
learning to dramatically change risk profiles of everyday events.

Machine learning has a lot of potential for risk management, but like
other technological advances, also brings some areas of concern. One of
the main areas of concern is that machine learning is a black-box technology; that is, it is not always possible to ascertain how a machine learning
algorithm makes the decisions that it does. This, of course, has the potential for unintended consequences. As a somewhat trivial example that you
may have experienced, perhaps you have used a voice recognition system
for typing some of your documents or e-mails. If so, then you know that
no matter how diligently you trained your voice recognition software, you
still need to carefully proofread the material for instances where the voice
recognition algorithm embarrassingly misinterpreted your voice.

While voice recognition is a relatively primitive form of machine
learning, and the mistakes caused by voice recognition are relatively tame,
the reality is that machine learning is more and more becoming a part
of our lives and other consequences of relying on black-box technology
may not be so benign. For instance, there have been several instances of
machine learning having unintended embedded biases based on race, or
even traits based on a person's Internet browser history. Furthermore, the
prospect of a nefarious hacker reconfiguring a piece of machine learning
software is a concern.

One interesting application of AI for nonprofits is using the technology to more efficiently match beneficiaries to nonprofits. Often, there is
a confusing mix of nonprofits with overlapping and sometimes competing objectives. This is particularly the case when it comes to the interface
between nonprofits and governmental agencies. A case in point is that of
immigration where a portfolio of nonprofits, combined with a portfolio
of governmental agencies can create a confusing maze for the intended

---

[2]https://www.nhtsa.gov/sites/nhtsa.dot.gov/files/documents/13069a-ads2.0_090617_
v9a_tag.pdf (accessed July 6, 2019).

beneficiaries. A particular case of this was observed during the Syrian refugee crisis in 2015. For instance, in Canada, a governmental aim was to increase the intake of refugees, but the mix and interfacing of various branches of governments with nonprofits made the government's objectives difficult to achieve despite significant resources committed to the project. Project planning and coordination aided by AI has promise for significantly reducing waste and overlap and increasing overall efficiency.[3]

Ultimately, machine learning and AI holds a lot of promise for risk management. Even given the unintended embedded biases, the reality is that a machine learning system will not only make fewer mistakes but also have less built-in bias than even the most diligently bias-free person. Bots, powered by machine learning, can also greater help with the efficiency of operations for a nonprofit and perhaps significantly reduce the complement of staff and volunteers needed. Machine learning-enabled bots are transforming the for-profit world and there is no reason to believe that the same will not be true for nonprofits as well.

Related to machine learning is fintech, which also goes by a variety of other terms including humantech. Fintech is the bringing together of machine learning, the IoT, and data collection to automate and manage many administrative tasks through bots or the use of computers. Again, fintech brings with it a set of positive and negative risks. The big positive is that many different aspects of fintech can greatly ease the burden on administrative tasks. Automated payment systems for instance, dramatically reduce the workload of the treasurer and other financially related staff of a nonprofit. Routine chores such as collecting admission fees can now all be done online or with other forms of electronic payments. The security concerns, and the handling of money issues have all but disappeared. Mailing lists and stuffing envelopes by hand is another common chore that has all but disappeared. Fintech is still at the very early stages

---

[3]Vectors Group, a Canadian management consulting company, of which one of the authors of this book is the Founder as well as a Lead Consultant, presented the CAN-I Project as an AI-based immigrant integration solution during National Metropolis Conference in Halifax in March 2019. CAN-I stands for Canada Immigrant Integration but also refers to the most used question by immigrants (CAN I find a job? How CAN I send my children to school? CAN I go to a doctor? etc.; www.VectorsGroup.ca).

of development and lots of interesting applications are sure to appear in the near future.

The issue with fintech is that it is only as good as the data analysis, the machine learning, and the IoT devices that it is connected to. All of the issues that belong to those aspects of technology, will also necessarily by extension belong to fintech.

Ultimately, we believe that technology is a strong positive for nonprofits, and that nonprofits should prudently take advantage of technology as they are able. The point is that technology always brings its own new positive and negatives and unintended consequences. Technology needs to be risk managed, and that risk management task is growing in urgency and importance.

Complexity

The second major trend that we observe is that of increasing complexity in the management of all types of organizations. This was a point that we have previously emphasized, and in several different places, but like data risk, it is a point that is worth repeating and exploring a bit further. You will recall that complexity arises in situations where there are agents, who can interact, and who can each adapt their behavior. Furthermore, unless there is an underlying set of laws that govern the interaction, the result can be the phenomenon of emergence. Emergence is a leaderless, and unpredictable set of patterns and outcomes that cannot be replicated or completely understood.

Complexity by itself is not necessarily a bad thing. But it does change the task of the manager. Instead of solving or optimizing issues, like one does with a complicated situation, the manager needs to think in terms of managing a situation. Some managers are very good at doing so, but other managers are more comfortable dealing with familiar and complicated type of situations where they have reasonable assurance that certain actions will produce certain outcomes.

Technology, and in particular social media, along with many other factors such as globalization, are catalysts for the increase in complexity. The ways of connecting and the ease and speed which one can do so have increased greatly the amount of complexity in the management task. No organization is an island anymore: even those that operate in a well-defined space for the benefit of a well-defined audience, such as many nonprofits do. Even the most seemingly innocent of actions are likely to be scrutinized and if in some way found wanting by someone, they will likely be publicized.

Complexity, if viewed as a risk, can be a good thing or a bad thing. Emergence can work for or against a nonprofit. For instance, the ice-bucket challenge in 2014 was such a great success for raising funds and awareness for amyotrophic lateral sclerosis (ALS). This challenge, which was based on social media friends challenging each other to record and post themselves dumping a bucket of ice and water over themselves in support of ALS, was an example of complexity and emergence creating a viral campaign that was hugely successful. However, it just as quickly become relatively irrelevant shortly thereafter. Indeed, a backlash started against the campaign for a variety of reasons including claims that it crowded out funding for other charities, did little to actually advance awareness of the disease, trivialized the disease by it being a useless stunt, it wasted water, and was even claimed to have negative health effects for some participants including death.

The ice-bucket challenge is a clear example of the increasing complexity caused by technology and social media. Social media, and the associated social media presence, created a viral emergence that quickly made the challenge a global phenomenon, and just as quickly faded away to nothing. It is hard to envision how such a boom–bust cycle could occur so rapidly without the catalyst of social media. However, such viral phenomena are now almost commonplace; Gangnam Style videos, fidget spinners, the latest cat video, and so on.

We see complexity increasing. Technology cannot alleviate complexity. (Technology also increases complexity in the conventional definition of the word as well.) In fact, there is a danger that technology is assumed to be a savior, or a fix, for risk management. For instance, a lot of risk management is now being managed by artificial intelligence. As the predicted accident reduction by the use of autonomous cars shows, AI may have significant advantages for managing certain types of risks. However, AI is only suited for managing complicated type risks. Until AI can learn to recognize and adapt to complexity like a human, there will be a need to have a human element to managing complex risks.

In a world that is increasingly global, and globally connected, the existence of complexity and emergence is always present. Like technology itself, complexity is not necessarily a bad risk or a good risk. However, it is a risk that needs to be managed and that risk management need is one that we see increasing into the foreseeable future.

Other Trends

While technology and complexity are what we consider to be the two most impactful risk management trends for nonprofits, there are a host of other trends that are also significant. The mere speed of risk is one of these trends. Again, technology and complexity are root causes of what is causing the speed of risk to increase.

The speed of risk has implications that risk management becomes a more dynamic activity. Risk management is no longer a safety manual that gets read when one joins an organization. Risk is ever changing, and risk policies, risk ideas, and risk thinking needs to constantly change with a similar pace. The speed of risk means that risk management needs to be a cultural priority, rather than a centralized authority. Risk cannot, and will not, wait for quarterly board meetings to have policies discussed and approved.

Those organizations with a positive risk culture that implement risk management policies but balances that with providing stakeholders with the tools, accountability, and responsibility for judgment to make informed and intelligent risk decisions are the ones that are successful. Decentralizing risk will undoubtedly lead to risk mistakes, but we argue that with the increasing pace of risk, that not decentralizing risk management will lead to even more bad risk decisions. The speed of risk is too great to manage without a positive risk culture and having all stakeholders of the nonprofit as part of risk management.

Risk management as a subject area is another trend that has arisen dramatically over the last 20 years. A variety of factors have contributed to this, but the growth of risk management awareness has changed the level of expectations around risk management.

Risk awareness arises from many different factors, but social media is one major contributing factor. Social media increases the transparency of the actions of an organization, and speeds communication when the actions of the organization are deemed "postable" on social media.

As risk managers, we, of course, welcome the increase focus on risk. However, too much of anything can become a negative, and this is true for risk management as well. A theme throughout this book has been that risk is "the possibility that bad or good things may happen." Too frequently, however, risk awareness is only focused on negative risk, to the detriment of the overall objectives of an organization. We believe that the trend of risk awareness needs to be balanced with a focus on the positive outcomes of the organization. Risk awareness thus, and ironically, becomes a risk that needs to be managed.

With increased risk awareness comes increasing levels of regulation. Governments react to public sentiment, and as public sentiment trends toward more risk awareness, so does government regulation. As previously discussed, regulation is both a risk, and a risk management device. However, regulatory management should almost never be taken to be risk management. The aims and objectives of regulators are very different from the aims and objectives of the nonprofits that they are regulating. In our experience, regulators are focused on downside risk, while nonprofits need to manage both downside and upside risks. Relatedly, is the increasing need for stakeholder management. While regulators are an important stakeholder, the other stakeholders as well are becoming more risk aware.

The last major trend that we see is the increasing level of collaboration and competition between nonprofit organizations. For-profit organizations, almost by definition, are in competition with each other. However, nonprofits should try to find a way to form partnerships of collaboration rather than competition whenever possible. However, it is inevitable that competition will also arise in the securement of resources and perhaps even in the area of servicing of beneficiaries. Competition and collaboration between nonprofit organizations can happen at three different contexts: geographic, service based, and supportive.

Technology has made coordination across geographic boundaries much easier. By forming alliances—particularly across boundaries, nonprofits can share not only resources but also ideas and best practices. Forming alliances, particularly across distance, does require extra managerial attention, but reduction in risks can be found not only by sharing ideas and resources but also by the portfolioing or sharing of risks. Geographic collaboration can be achieved by national or international associations, coalitions, or government organizations that regulate the roles and pools resources to create a set of best practices.

Service-based partnerships are instances where the service of one nonprofit organization can support the service of another one. For example, a nonprofit organization that provides employment support services to the immigrants can collaborate with a nonprofit language school.

The competition and overlaps are also possible in terms of services. If nonprofit organizations are geographically apart the overlaps are preferred. But if they are in the same region any overlap basically may mean unnecessary competition and waste of limited resources.

Federal, state, or local governments or big funding organizations can manage the services in their areas to avoid unnecessary overlaps. Considering that there are around 1.3 million nonprofit organizations in the United States where each nonprofit offer 3 to 10 different kinds of services, it is almost impossible for governments and funding organizations to optimize the whole system without the support of smart technologies using machine learning and data analytics. By taking a collaborative approach, access to funding sources may be improved, leading to reduced financial risks.

Concluding Thoughts

Ultimately, we believe that risk management will become more important in the day-to-day operations of nonprofits; at least that is how we interpret the trends. Technology is increasing the expectations of what can be done with risk management. Social media is increasing the transparency as well as both speeding up and increasing the breadth of knowledge of risk missteps. Data availability is giving the general public as well as regulators the information that they need to impose greater regulatory as well as socially conscious reforms.

All of this increases the expectations and the possibilities of good risk management for nonprofits. It is our sincere hope that this book is a useful step on the way to making that more risk intelligent future a reality for your nonprofit.

About the Authors

Rick Nason, PhD, CFA, is a risk consultant and an associate professor of finance at Dalhousie University, Halifax, Canada. Dr. Nason has advised and developed programs on risk management, risk measurement, and risk strategy for both large and small corporations, international financial institutions, and governmental agencies. He is also an active member on several nonprofit boards.

Omer Livvarcin, PhD, is the founder and CEO of Vectors Group, a consulting and training company specialized in nonprofit and social enterprises. Besides consulting, Omer also has strong ties to academia, holding positions at the Telfer School of Management at the University of Ottawa, as part-time professor, and the Nonprofit Management Laboratory, researcher. He has developed several quantitative models and metrics for strategic impact management in nonprofit organizations.

Index

AI. *See* Artificial intelligence (AI)
ALS. *See* Amyotrophic lateral sclerosis
 (ALS)
Amyotrophic lateral sclerosis
 (ALS), 169
Apple managers, 126
Artificial intelligence (AI), 23–24,
 166, 167
ATMs. *See* Automated teller machines
 (ATMs)
Automated teller machines
 (ATMs), 24

Balancing operating, 86–87
BEST model, 122–124
Best-selling musician, 13
Biden Cancer Institute, 107
Biden, Joe, 107
#BlackLivesMatter, 108
Boundary management, 150
Boundary shifts, 151–152
Boy Scouts, 108
Burn rate, 81–82
Bush, George W., 2

Canadian charity, 140
Capital budgeting, 82–83
Caution Zone, 103
Challenging risk decisions, 27
Check Engine Soon, 67, 68
Civica Rx, 136
Cognitive diversity, 48
Coin-flipping game, 25–26
Coin-tossing game, 26
Committee of Sponsoring
 Organizations of the
 Treadway Commission, 7
Complacency Zone, 103
Complex problems, 13
Complex systems, 12, 13
Complex versus complicated, 55–56
Complexity, 168–170

Complexity management, 18
Complexity risk, 12–14
Complexity science, 12–14
Compliance management, 5
Complicated systems, 13
Control environment, 5
COSO frameworks, 32–34
Crisis management, 4
Critical situations, escalation for,
 158–159

D&O insurance, 105–106
Danger Zone risk, 102
Danish company, 136
Data analysis, 61, 62
Data principles, 60–62
Day-to-day operations, xiii, 95, 163
Deaf youth, 93
Delphi Method, 65–66
Designated swimming areas, 20–21
Directors' legal risk, 104–106
Drucker's, Peter, 62
Duke, Annie, 85
Dynamics change, 15

Effective risk management, 11
Enjoying, reasonable rules of, 21
Enron, 32
Entrepreneurial firms, 81
Ethical guidelines, 107
Ethics, 106–111
Ethics handbook, 109–110
External risk communication,
 157–158
External versus internal risks, 54–55

Financial data analysis, 75
Financial risks, 51–52
 balancing operating, 86–87
 burn rate, 81–82
 capital budgeting, 82–83
 five-year financial risk, 80–81

Financial risks (*continued*)
    forecasting uncertainty, 76–79
    funding risk, 85–87
    introduction to, 75
    scenario analysis, 79–80
    stress analysis, 79–80
    working capital management,
        83–84
Financial variability, 78
Fintech, 167–168
Firm, 6, 9, 21, 28, 33, 42, 81, 82, 93,
        111, 155
Five-year financial risk, 80–81
Forecasting uncertainty, 76–79
Functional diversity, 48
Funding risk, 85–87
Fuzzy thinking, 40

Good outcomes, 7
Green Zone risks, 119–120

Heat map, 119
Human capital risk, 53–54, 92–93
Human resources, 96
Hurricane Katrina, 94
Hydro One, 6–7

Ice-bucket challenge, 169
Identifying risks, 65–67
Ineffective risk governance, 160–161
Information technology (IT), 93–95
Infrastructure risk, 93–95
Internal management versus
        outsourcing risk management,
        125–127
Internal risk communication, 157
Internet browser history, 166
Internet of Things (IoT), 164,
        167, 168
IoT. *See* Internet of Things (IoT)
ISO frameworks, 32–34
IT. *See* Information technology (IT)

Japanese garden, 22

Katheryn's Situation, 146–148
Keynes, John Maynard, 41

Lam, James, 5

Lance Armstrong Foundation,
        52–53, 56
Legal, compliance/reputational risks
    directors' legal risk, 104–106
    ethics, 106–111
    introduction to, 101–104
    reputational risk, 111–112
Lemay, Kathryn, 133–135, 146–148
Lifeguard resources, 21
Light, Paul, 95
Little-League Baseball, 49, 77
Little-League nonprofit, 83
Lopez, Tomas, 20, 21, 90–91

Machine learning, 165–166
Madoff, Bernie, 106
Management, sounding-board for,
        159–160
Manchester Bidwell Corporation, 140
Mathematical algorithm/theory, 18
Measuring risks, 65–67
#MeToo, 55, 108
Myths, risk management, 17–22

Negative outcomes, 7
Nonprofit organizations, risks of
    complex versus complicated, 55–56
    directors, spin-off effect to, 104
    external versus internal risks, 54–55
    financial risk, 51–52
    human capital risk, 53–54
    introduction to, 45–46
    legal risk, 54
    operational risk, 51
    reputational risk, 52–53
    risk identification of, 46–48
    risk management, first law of,
        46–48
    strategic risk, 48–51
Nova Scotia school board, 113, 126,
        127

Operating capital, 83
Operational processes, 90–91
Operational risk zones, 95–97
Operational risks
    human capital risk, 92–93
    infrastructure risk, 93–95
    introduction to, 89–90

operational processes, 90–91
operational risk zones, 95–97
risk culture, 98–99
training, 98

Partnership risk management, 135
Partnerships/stakeholder engagement
introduction to, 133–135
Katheryn's Situation, 146–148
nature of, 135–136
stakeholder risks, 144–145
stakeholder trio, 142–144
vector model, 136–142
Passive activity, 14–15
Phoenix-based charity, 86
Ponzi scheme, 106
Provincial Chief Medical Officer, 127

Rear-view mirror, 3
Red Cross, 94–95
Red Zone risks, 119–120
RegTech, 102
Reputational risk, 52–53, 54,
    111–112
Resources, allocation of, 122
Risk
definition of, 1–4
introduction to, 1–4, 17
strategic evaluation of, 115
strategy and mission, 28
Risk analytics
data principles, 60–62
identifying risks, 65–67
introduction to, 59–60
measuring risks, 65–67
risk dashboards, 67–68
risk maps, 62–64
risk radars, 68–70
risk registers/risk evolution, 72–73
risk scenarios/backcasting, 71
risk scores, 73
Risk appetite, 116–119
Risk communication, 157–158
Risk culture, 98–99
Risk dashboard design, 158
Risk dashboards, 67–68
Risk governance
boundary management, 150
boundary shifts, 151–152

critical situations, escalation for,
    158–159
hierarchy of, 152–153
introduction to, 149–150
management, sounding-board for,
    159–160
risk communication, 157–158
risk dashboard design, 158
specific risk activities, 153–156
symptoms of, 160–161
Risk identification, 46–48
Risk investment, return on, 124–125
Risk management
active, not a passive activity, 14–15
adoption of, 8
art/science, 29
basic steps of, 9–11
benefits of, xiii
complex problems, 13
complexity risk, 12–14
complexity science, 12–14
create and implement, 5
"department of No!", 4, 6
design of, 25
first law of, 46–48
for-profit or nonprofit
    organizations, xi, 28
future of
    complexity, 168–170
    introduction to, 163
    technology and risk, 163–168
    trends, 170–172
implementing of, xi, 7, 9, 11
important factors in, 18
introduction to, 4–6
myths, 17–22
primary function of, 7
risks of, xii
risk appetite, 155–156
risk tolerance, 155–156
set objectives for, 154–155
six advantages of, 7–8
of strategic activity, 6–7
truths, 22–28
value-added activity, 7–9
Risk management frameworks
COSO and ISO frameworks,
    32–34
introduction to, 31–32

Risk management frameworks
    (*continued*)
  risk management tower, 42–43
  risk management trio, 40–41
  stakeholder trio, 41–42
  ViStA core, 39–40
  ViStA risk framework, 34–39
Risk management tower, 31, 38–39,
    42–43
Risk maps, 36, 62–64, 65, 119–120
Risk parameters trio, 35–37
Risk radars, 68–70
Risk registers/risk evolution, 72–73
Risk responses, 127–130
Risk scenarios/backcasting, 71
Risk scores, 73
Risk-specific terminology, 37
Risk threshold, 120–121
Risk tolerance, 116–119
Risk treatment
  BEST model, 122–124
  internal management versus
      outsourcing risk management,
      125–127
  introduction to, 113–114
  resources, allocation of, 122
  risk appetite, 116–119
  risk investment, return on,
      124–125
  risk map, 119–120
  risk responses, 127–130
  risk threshold, 120–121
  risk tolerance, 116–119
  strategic evaluation of risk, 115
Risk versus Strategies matrix, 116
Roxbury Comprehensive Community
    Clinic, 105
Rugby Nova Scotia, 129
Rumsfeld, Donald, 2, 3, 27

Safety systems, 25
Sarbanes–Oxley Act (SOX), 32
Scenario analysis, 79–80
Science, 17, 18, 29
Scientists, 12

Self-driving automobiles, 23–24
Social media, 53, 54, 111, 165
Social sciences, 13
SOX. *See* Sarbanes–Oxley Act (SOX)
Specific risk activities, 153–156
Spin-off effect, 104
Stakeholder risks, 144–145
Stakeholder trio, 37–38, 41–42,
    142–144
Stakeholders, xiii, 9, 11, 24, 26, 38,
    49, 52, 65, 66, 76, 90, 99,
    103, 107, 116–117, 139
Strategic activity, 6–7
Strategic evaluation of risk, 115
Strategic objectives, 5, 9
Strategic plan, 6–7
Strategic risk, 48–51
Stress analysis, 79–80
Syrian refugee crisis, 167

Technology and risk, 163–168
Training, 98
Trends, 170–172
Truths, risk management, 22–28

Value-added activity, 6, 7–9
Vector model, 136–142
ViStA core, 34–35, 39, 42
ViStA risk framework, 32, 34–39
Volatility, uncertainty, complexity,
    and ambiguity (VUCA), 29
Volunteer Protection Act (VPA), 105
VPA. *See* Volunteer Protection Act
    (VPA)
VUCA. *See* Volatility, uncertainty,
    complexity, and ambiguity
    (VUCA)

Wikipedia page, 3
Working capital management,
    83–84
World Trade Center, 117
Worldcom, 32

Yellow Zone risks, 120

OTHER TITLES IN OUR FINANCE AND FINANCIAL MANAGEMENT COLLECTION

John Doukas, Old Dominion University, *Editor*

Announcing the Business Expert Press Digital Library

www.ingramcontent.com/pod-product-compliance
Lightning Source LLC
Chambersburg PA
CBHW061307220326
41599CB00026B/4774